Renaissance Galway

DELINEATING THE
SEVENTEENTH-CENTURY CITY

Paul Walsh

D1611167

Comhairle Cathrach na Gaillimhe
Galway City Council

Acadamh Ríoga na hÉireann
Royal Irish Academy

First published in 2019
by the Irish Historic Towns Atlas
Royal Irish Academy
19 Dawson Street
Dublin 2

www.ria.ie

in association with
Galway City Council (www.galwaycity.ie)
City Hall, Galway

ISBN 978-1-911479-07-9

Irish Historic Towns Atlas series editors: H.B. Clarke, Raymond Gillespie, Jacinta Prunty, Michael Potterton; consultant editors: J.H. Andrews, Anngret Simms; cartographic editor: Sarah Gearty; editorial assistants: Jennifer Moore, Frank Cullen.

British Library Cataloguing-in-Publication Data. A catalogue record is available from the British Library.

Design: Fidelma Slattery.

Printed in Poland by BZGraf S.A.

Royal Irish Academy is a member of Publishing Ireland, the Irish book publishers' association.

10 9 8 7 6 5 4 3 2 1

To the people of Galway

CONTENTS

CONTENTS

This book is one of a number of ancillary publications to the Irish Historic Towns Atlas. These are intended to make available material relevant to published atlas fascicles. This volume accompanies Irish Historic Towns Atlas, no. 28, *Galway/Gaillimh* by Jacinta Prunty and Paul Walsh. It explores a unique piece of Irish cartographical history, the pictorial map of mid-seventeenth-century Galway, a photographic reproduction of which is contained in the fascicle together with a transcript of the reference tables.

Renaissance Galway is a joint publication between the Royal Irish Academy and Galway City Council. The author and editors are especially grateful to Professor Michael Clarke who very kindly provided translations of the Latin text and to Dr Nollaig Ó Muraíle for advice in relation to Irish name forms. Dr Peter Van der Krogt generously commented on issues relating to where the map was printed and Meeno Leenstra shared his expertise of seventeenth-century Dutch shipping. Thanks are due to the staff in the Manuscripts and Archives Research Library, Trinity College, Dublin, and the Special Collections section of the James Hardiman Library, NUI Galway, for facilitating the study of the maps in their collections; and to Gillian Whelan, Senior Photographer, Digital Resources and Imaging Department, Trinity College, Dublin. The author wishes to express his warmest appreciation to Kieran Hoare (Special Collections, NUI Galway) and Paul Ferguson and Paul Mulligan (Glucksman Map Library, Trinity College, Dublin) for their help and assistance. Timothy Collins, former chartered librarian at NUI Galway and John Gillis, Conservation Department, Trinity College Library, kindly provided information on the conservation of the map in the James Hardiman Library, NUI Galway. Unless otherwise credited, all photographs are from the author's collection.

H.B. Clarke, Raymond Gillespie, Jacinta Prunty, Michael Potterton
Editors, Irish Historic Towns Atlas, Royal Irish Academy

PREFACE

The extracts included in this book have been taken from the map in Trinity College, Dublin (MS 1209/73), and they are reproduced with the permission of the Board of Trinity College. The composite photograph of the copy in Galway is reproduced courtesy of the James Hardiman Library, NUI Galway. The extract from the surveys of Thomas Sherrard (1785) is reproduced courtesy of the Board of Governors of the Schools founded by Erasmus Smith Esq.

The map extracts are numbered **1–38**. Numbers in bold in the text provide a cross-reference to a relevant extract and commentary. The numbers in italics reference the letter, number or signum used in the original map and visible in the extract.

Commentaries on items of generic interest relating to the map are presented first (nos **1–7**). The order of the ensuing extracts reflects that presented in the map's two tables of reference, the *Elenchus* and the *Synopsis*. Matters pertaining to the walled town (nos **8–23**) precede those on the east (nos **24–30**) and west (nos **31–38**) sides of the river respectively. An index to the various extracts is provided inside the front cover.

Biblical quotations recorded on the map follow the Latin Vulgate edition sanctioned by Pope Clement VIII in 1592. This was the standard Bible text of the Roman Catholic Church until 1979 and the numbering of the psalms follows this edition. To convey a sense of contemporary equivalence, the English translations are taken from the Douay–Rheims *Holy Bible* (1635 reprint).

In the introduction and commentaries accompanying the map extracts, the building and street names, unless otherwise indicated, are standardised to those used in Irish Historic Towns Atlas, no. 28, *Galway/Gaillimh* by Jacinta Prunty and Paul Walsh.

EDITORIAL NOTE

AES	Archive of the Schools founded by Erasmus Smith, Dublin.
BL	British Library, London.
GCCA	Galway County Council Archives.
JHL	James Hardiman Library, National University of Ireland, Galway.
JGAHS	*Journal of the Galway Archaeological and Historical Society.*
NLI	National Library of Ireland.
NMS	National Monuments Service, Department of Culture, Heritage and the Gaeltacht.
NUI	National University of Ireland.
TCD	Trinity College, Dublin.
TNA:PRO	The National Archives: Public Record Office, London.

ABBREVIATIONS

LIST OF ILLUSTRATIONS

Part I ~ Introduction

Fig. 1: Composite image of the map in the James Hardiman Library, NUI Galway (JHL).

THE PICTORIAL MAP
OF MID-SEVENTEENTH-CENTURY GALWAY:
AN OVERVIEW

Galway is unique among Irish cities in possessing a map that not just provides a bird's-eye view of the urban landscape at a critical juncture in its history but also offers insights into the cultural, sociopolitical and religious outlooks of the town's ruling elite at this time. This printed map is a glorification of Galway, a celebration of its importance, wealth and power in the years immediately preceding its surrender to parliamentary forces in 1652. That it was made to impress is evinced not only in the visual impact of the heraldic embellishments and decorative artistry employed but also in the wealth of detail recorded, much of which might otherwise remain unknown. Only two copies of the original published map are known to exist, one in the James Hardiman Library, NUI Galway,[1] and the other in the library of Trinity College, Dublin (MS 1209/73).[2] Its significance has long been recognised since James Hardiman first brought it to general notice in his *History of Galway* published in 1820.[3]

Although unique in terms of its subject matter, the pictorial map fits readily within the canon of printed wall maps that were very popular among the social elites throughout Europe in the sixteenth and seventeenth centuries. Measuring a little over 2 m (6 feet 7 inches) by 1.4 m (4 feet 6 inches) the map comprises nine sheets in three rows. The individual sheets would have been stuck together to form a single composite image and then, usually mounted on fabric, attached to turned wooden rollers at the top and bottom to facilitate hanging. This impressive map would have graced the walls of offices and dwellings of wealthy Galway merchants and landowners in much the same manner as those depicted in the paintings of domestic interiors by the Dutch masters of this period.[4]

Wall maps operated both as 'map' and 'work of art' as the blend of the cartographic and the aesthetic resulted in a very decorative outcome that was certain to elicit appreciation. In this regard, many of these maps were varnished to display them to maximum effect and in the mistaken belief that this would protect them from light and dirt. They were subject also to deterioration as a result of smoke from fires, light, dampness, dirt and general handling by interested parties; this probably accounts for the fact that only two copies of the Galway map survive.[5] The copy in the James Hardiman Library was coated with varnish and, as the upper and lower edges still retain the holes where it had been tacked to batons or rollers, there is little doubt that it had been hanging on a wall.[6] The copy in TCD library, on the other hand, appears to have survived as individual sheets until mounted on fabric in 1816 and this would account for its exceptionally good condition.[7] It is impossible to know how many copies of the map were printed but, considering its specific local content, probably a small number only. Several are recorded as hanging in the homes of wealthy Galway merchants in 1684 (see below) and others undoubtedly were purchased by those who had moved from the town to the country following the Commonwealth expulsions and transplantations.[8]

The design and layout of the various elements on the map draw on a long tradition of Renaissance cartographical imagery and

INTRODUCTION

archetypes. While no specific model has been identified to date, John Speed's 'Invasions' map of Great Britain and Ireland (published 1603–4) or the county maps in his *Theatre* (published 1611[12]) may have provided the seminal inspiration for the inclusion of heraldic shields and labels along the borders.[9] The choice of the elevated or bird's-eye perspective – similar to Speed's map of the town, dated 1610,[10] – was intentional in that it allowed the compilers to present a holistic view of the town as a complete self-contained and internally organised entity. At the same time it enhanced the viewer's appreciation of its setting in the landscape.[11] The wide visual field adopted for this perspective encompassed a broad stretch of the topography surrounding the town which, in order to fit within the available map space, has led to inconsistencies in the relative orientation of individual elements and some contraction and distortion. The viewer should note that the map is not aligned like modern maps that have north at the top: in this case, as indicated by its compass rose (visible in **30**), north is towards the bottom left-hand quadrant.

***

Although Galway's economic success was built on a spirit of mercantile enterprise, by the middle of the seventeenth century its ruling elite had secured for themselves extensive estates throughout Connacht.[12] Their members had risen to prominence in local and national politics[13] and had been appropriately rewarded with knighthoods and baronetcies for their loyalty to the crown. Of the ten named individuals whose town houses are identified on the map, five were knights and two were baronets (see **6**).[14] Being Catholic in disposition and outlook, a number of townsmen had been elevated to senior positions in the church.[15] Others, despite the handicap of their religious affiliation, rose to prominence in the legal profession.[16] Inevitably this brought them into contact with members of the Old English aristocratic houses with whom they formed alliances. These familial connections are highlighted on the right and left borders of the map that showcase twenty-three unnamed (i.e., the cartouches are blank) armorial bearings of distinguished families aligned with those of Galway.[17] Pride of place, however, was reserved for the armorial achievements of their own fourteen principal families and their associated ancestral lineages, which are displayed along the bottom border in three interlinked cartouches (see **2**).

The bottom left- and right-hand sheets are dominated by two extensive tables of reference, titled respectively *Elenchus* (left) and *Synopsis* (right). Between them they contain 267 entries (149 in the *Elenchus* and 118 in the *Synopsis*). The former references features of interest within the town and the latter, divided into two parts, *In orientem* and *In occidentem*, refers to items on the east and west sides of the river respectively. Latin, the Renaissance *lingua franca* of scholarly, clerical and international audiences, is used throughout for the textual element.[18] In some instances English or Irish names have been included, especially where the common form of a placename is recorded. As might be expected, a greater number of Irish placenames are documented outside the walled town. Nonetheless, the common names of a number of the wall towers and streets are in Irish (e.g., Tor an Leoin – the Lion Tower; Sráid Tobar an Iarla – Earl Street). To what extent these indicate the widespread use of the Irish language in mid-seventeenth-century Galway or are merely a survival of earlier forms, much as Bohermore continues in use today, is unknown.[19] Nonetheless, it is reasonable to suggest that Irish was the spoken tongue of not only the general populace outside the walls but of many within as well.[20]

The earliest-known historical reference to the existence of the map occurs among the writings of two members of the well-known Molyneux family of Dublin. When Thomas Molyneux was studying in Holland in 1684, his elder brother William wrote to him from Dublin: 'I hear that the citizens of Galway, about 20 or 30 years ago, got a large map of Galway printed at Antwerp, where perhaps you may light on one, if you lay out for it. Pray, Tom, endeavor it, for I would fain receive a copy thereof. There are several in the merchants' houses in Galway, hung up in their halls, but I fear none to be procurable from them'.[21] As Mitchell has pointed out,[22] it is not known whether Thomas Molyneux obtained a copy but William's son, Samuel, succeeded in procuring one at Galway when he visited the town in 1709: 'Having view'd the town, I was directed where I might have a map of it, which I bought, and seems pretty exact: 'twas done at Brussells by a fryer who was born and bred in the town, and they tell you, had been at Brussells 8 years when he made it'.[23] There is little doubt but that the map in question is the pictorial map of Galway.

The next reference to this map is to be found among the writings of the historian of the Dominican order in Ireland, Thomas Burke

INTRODUCTION

(d. 1776). Writing in 1772 in the *Supplementum* to his *Hibernia Dominicana* (1762), he gives a brief description of the map and quotes the verses from the bottom border. He first saw this copy as a young man (*quam adolescentulus*) in St Isidore's College, Rome, which suggests that he was given access to it *c.* 1725–30.[24] This copy cannot now be traced[25] though it was consulted there by Fr Valentine Bodkin who, in a letter dated 21 January 1796, records it as the 'Galway map, which still exists here, and is nearly destroyed, . . . it's torn, it's erased, and whitewashed in some places. One Fr Bermingham, a learned Galway Franciscan[26] . . . procured and left it to the Convent. . . . it's better than 6 feet'.[27]

A passing reference in a letter written by Edward Willes, chief baron of the Irish exchequer, suggests that he saw a copy in Galway while on circuit there *c.* 1760. Having referred to Galway's connection with the crown through the marriage of the daughter of the earl of Ulster with Lionel, duke of Clarence, he states: 'In a very ancient map of Galway his palace makes a magnificent figure, but nothing now remains of it'.[28] It seems likely that the map in question is the pictorial map and the 'palace' may be identified with the *vetera aedificia*, the 'old buildings of the illustrious lord, Richard de Burgo, the Red Earl', listed in the index (see **13**).

William Molyneux's comments are especially pertinent in identifying where the map is likely to have been printed. By the middle of the sixteenth century Antwerp had become the major European centre for commercial cartography. The conquest by Spain of the southern provinces in the mid-1580s meant that in the ensuing decades the focus of production largely shifted to Amsterdam in the north, which became the centre of wall-map production in the following century.[29] That said, this map does not appear to have come from any of its major cartographical publishing houses[30] and, more than likely, was printed in the southern provinces which were controlled by Catholic Spain.[31] Another reason to support the printing of the map in this area is the presence there of Fr Henry Joyce, who has been identified as the person who 'finished, blazoned and described' the work.[32] He concealed his identity under his initials in the map's dedicatory inscription, which is contained in the cartouche immediately below the royal coat of arms of Charles II: *Augustissimo faustissimoque suo principi, Carolo II, Dei gratia, Angliae, Scotiae, Franciae & Hiberniae regi, serenissimo, &c. ab adictissimo suae majestatis cliente,*

R.D.H.I. istius urbis cive & pastore oblata. Civitatem, et se, suaque omnia, in, et extra urbem, D.O.M. & SSᵉ S Mᵗⁱ aeterno voto consecrat, dedicatque S.P.Q.G. (Offered to his most August, Auspicious and Serene Highness, Charles II, by the grace of God, king of England, Scotland, France and Ireland etc., from your Majesty's most devoted subject, R.D.H.I., citizen and pastor of that city. The senate and people of Galway consecrate and dedicate the citizenry and themselves and all their possessions both within and without the city to God, Most Good, Most Great and to his Most Serene and Sacred Majesty by an everlasting vow).

Hardiman identified the initials R.D.H.I. as those of the Revd Fr Henry Joyce (*Reverendissimus Dominus Henricus Ioyce*).[33] Fr Joyce was a vicar of the collegiate church of St Nicholas in the 1630s and throughout the troubled times of the 1640s. Both he and his brother Gregory, also a vicar, continued to minister secretly in the town subsequent to its surrender in 1652. In 1654 or shortly after, they settled in the Spanish Low Countries together with their brother William, an army officer.[34] Four years later Henry was appointed pro-vicar of the Irish troops in the service of Charles II,[35] a factor that would have made him favourably disposed to the monarch. While his name is the only one directly associated with the production of this map, the presence on the Continent of so many Irish exiles during the 1650s would have provided an appropriate milieu and possibly support to facilitate its printing. The pronounced Catholic character of the work suggests a direct clerical input[36] and it is likely that Fr Joyce not only contributed to its content and final layout but may also have subsidised the cost of having it printed. Both he and his brothers were sufficiently wealthy to fund the building of a church at Louvain in 1659 for the Irish Dominican province, while Gregory Joyce financed the publication of the life of Francis Kirwan, bishop of Killala, written by his fellow townsman, Fr John Lynch, some ten years later.[37]

Whether or not Henry Joyce was the principal compiler of this massive undertaking cannot now be ascertained, but given the magnitude of the task it seems reasonable to suggest that it was not simply the work of one individual. That Fr Joyce was the prime figure in overseeing its publication is not in doubt although, with due humility, he placed only his initials on record. It seems very likely that others were involved and remain hidden behind the dedicatory initials S*[enatus]*

INTRODUCTION

Fig. 2: Cartouche containing the dedicatory inscription.

P[opulus] Q[que] G[alviae] – a play on the initialism S.P.Q.R. of Rome – in the map's dedication. The publication of such a work would not have been incompatible with the objectives of 'the comittie appointed by the auld and auncient freemen late of Gallway' that had been set up to lobby Charles II around the time of his restoration.[38] There is every reason to infer that it was supported by members of the various families whose town houses are referenced on it.[39]

Given that there are no contemporary historical references to its production and origin, it is necessary to look to the map itself to provide some of these answers. As with all printed texts, the meaning of this map is conditioned by the context in which it was created. An essential clue as to its nature and purpose is contained in the title. This is displayed in capital letters on an elongated ribbon directly below the top border: *Urbis Galviae totius Conatiae in regno Hiberniae clarissimae metropolis, et emporii celeberrimi delineatio historica* (An historical delineation of the city of Galway, the capital of Connacht in the kingdom of Ireland, the illustrious metropolis and renowned centre of commerce). The words *delineatio historica* (historical delineation) are important in that they clearly indicate to the reader the 'historical' framework employed in its composition. The blending of geography and history implies that everything illustrated is not, necessarily, accurately represented either in space or in time. For example, both St Augustine's Fort and church (see **24**), which are portrayed as extant on the map, had been pulled down by the time the parliamentary

army had erected the siege works to the east of the town, also shown on this map (see **27**). Although depicted as a completed structure, St Bridget's Chapel had never been finished (see **25**). In addition, the map incorrectly positions an entrance to the town beside the Lion Tower bastion (see **9**)[40] and, given the artistic nature of the work, every element of the fortifications (including the siege works) has been perfected and regularised with finely dressed ashlar masonry. These counterfeits are informative in providing insight into the intent of its compilers. This is not an example of cartographical realism but a multi-layered engagement with memory presented in pictorial form. The past is a commodity to be regenerated within a framework of visual imagery.[41] This important dimension is further highlighted in the heading of the *Elenchus* reference table where it is described as *hoc iconismo*, this 'picture' or 'image' rather than this 'map'.

In this regard, a distinguishing characteristic of this work is worthy of special attention: the recurrent reference to the number 'fourteen' and, more importantly, its factor 'seven',[42] that feature prominently in the content and indices. It undoubtedly mirrors the fourteen principal families identified on the bottom border as the founders of the town, the so-called 'tribes' of Galway (see **2**).[43] The verses below these explicitly emphasise the number 'fourteen', boasting that while Rome might have seven hills, the Nile seven mouths and the Pole seven stars, Galway – the Rome of Connacht[44] – not only has twice this number of illustrious families but 'twice seven'

INTRODUCTION

remarkable features that are listed in detail. The index lists seven ascents to the walls, seven open spaces and gardens, seven market places, fourteen fortifications, forts or ramparts around the walls, fourteen towers, fourteen gates, fourteen principal streets, fourteen lanes, fourteen religious residences, fourteen principal properties or castles and town houses, etc.[45] One suspects that accuracy may have fallen victim to numerical imperatives and it is impossible to verify the existence of everything mentioned. This is not to suggest that features or sites depicted on the map did not exist but rather that some minor features may have been exaggerated to appropriate proportions to complete the required number and others, perhaps, omitted so as not to exceed this chosen figure.[46] The use of this device serves to highlight one of the map's limitations and must caution the user against an uncritical acceptance of everything named or depicted.

A further insight into the ambition that inspired the map's creation may be inferred from the fact that it was not intended simply to serve as a stand-alone wall map but was planned to function as a pictorial reference to a series of volumes on Galway. Features are identified on the map by a number, letter or signum and these are referenced in the three indices where space has been left for the inclusion of book, chapter and folio number; abbreviated on the map to L.C.F. (*Liber, Capitulum, Folio*). Some idea of the comprehensive nature of these volumes can be gleaned from the extensive contents list in the oval compartment at the bottom centre of the map. Appropriately titled *Galviensis descriptionis declaratio* (The declaration of the description of Galway), the principal components of the work are 'declared' under fourteen headings and multiple sub-headings. This wide-ranging list of contents would not have been unusual at that time for a work of this nature. It is very much within the Renaissance

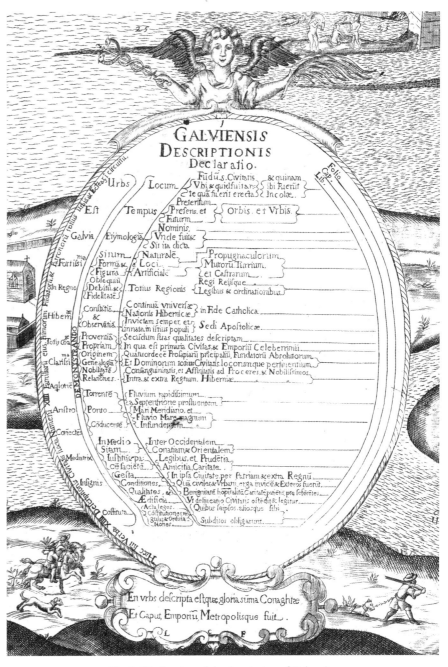

Fig. 3: 'Declaration of the description of Galway' – the index to the contents to the volumes that were intended to accompany the map.

INTRODUCTION

Fig. 4: In three of the medallions the king holds a commander's baton in his right hand. In the fourth – the second from the right (above) – the artist incorrectly depicts it in his left hand which, however, is engraved as a right arm attached to the left side of the king's body.

tradition in its ordering of knowledge according to standardised thematic headings. And, as if to further emphasise Galway's mercantile ancestry, the compartment is presided over by Victoria, the tutelary Roman goddess of victory. She holds the caduceus,[47] the symbol of commerce, and a palm frond, symbolising victory, triumph and peace. Again, lest the reader be in any doubt about the inclusion of this allegorical representation, the inscription in the cartouche underneath the compartment boasts that Galway is the glory of Connacht and its foremost commercial metropolis. Clearly, this map was intended to be a pictorial reference for an extensive chorographical account contained in a multi-volume work. What is significant is that the spaces where the book, chapter and folio numbers should be printed all remain blank. This would suggest that the map was brought into print before the other elements had been completed.[48]

The profuse dedication of the work to the restored monarch, Charles II, speaks of a connection that calls for particular exploration. The top border is devoted exclusively to a display of loyalty to this king. Four medallions containing emblematic depictions of the monarch on horseback dominate the frame[49] and the intervening spaces are filled with thirteen shields in three groups, nine of which are emblazoned with arms. Each shield is accompanied by a legend identifying the king's individual dominions.[50] The three groups are flanked by pairs of squat Tuscan columns proclaiming *Plus* (left) and *Ultra* (right), an allegorical reference to the Pillars of Hercules at the Strait of Gibraltar that marked the limits of the known classical world and, by implication, the boundaries of the king's domains.[51]

INTRODUCTION

Interspersed between the medallions and coats of arms is an inscription in large capital letters: *Heri, Hodie & in Secula*, an indirect allusion to St Paul's letter to the Hebrews (13:8): *Iesus Christus heri et hodie ipse et in saecula* (Jesus Christ, yesterday, and today: the same also for ever). The statement *Domino Consecratur Monarchia* (The monarchy is consecrated to the Lord) is printed directly below this in smaller capitals, signifying the ruler's position in the greater hierarchy. And lest the reader be in any doubt about the dedicatory subject, his name, *Carolus Rex*, is printed along the bottom of the border of the three top sheets. The underlying message is clear: this is an affirmation of the importance and centrality of monarchy in the natural, and divinely appointed, order of things.

To further highlight the significance of Charles II, the royal coat of arms occupies a prominent position at the centre of the upper of two rows of three shields near the top of the map (see **1**). It is flanked by two cartouches containing couplets extolling the allegiance of his subjects and their fervent desire for his future prosperity.

Terra, fretum, populi, quaeque aspicis undique late,
The land, the sea, the peoples, whatever you see on every side abroad,

Sunt tibi, sint generi, Carole, fida tuo.
They are faithful to you, Charles; and may they be faithful to your descendants.

Plus ultra tibi, quam tabule, vel continet orbis,
Beyond everything that charts or the world itself can contain,

Quae spheram superant suspice, nosce tua.
Things that surpass the globe – take them, know that they are yours.

As befitting loyal subjects, the three shields bearing the arms of Galway occupy a subordinate position below those of the king (see **1**) and the devotion of the former inhabitants to their monarch is flatteringly expressed further in the verses underneath each one:

Prima tuis proavis dedimus primordia nostre
Urbis, et infantes nosque serene tibi.
We gave the first origins of our city to your ancestors, and we give our children and ourselves, serene one, to you.

Galvia quam colimus vestra est, jam respice pictam;
Nos quoque sacramus nostraque nosque tibi.
The Galway that we venerate is yours, look now on its picture; we also consecrate our possessions and ourselves to you.

Flosque juventutis sub te crescentis abunde,
Est tuus, atque status, tempora, jura, bona.
And the flower of the young people, who flourish abundantly under you, is yours, and our situation, our times, our rights, our goods.

In addition to these explicit declarations of fealty the map includes a complementary language of deference that implicitly commemorates the royal personage. The two compartments containing the *Elenchus* and the *Synopsis* are surmounted by allegorical compositions (see **3**, **4**). These devices were not incorporated simply as ornamental frameworks – though they do serve this purpose – but rather invoke a shared cultural status through their use of Christian, especially Catholic, and classical motifs. This is the vocabulary of patronage whereby self-interest, imbued with higher motives, was articulated with imagery from classical and religious sources. The symbolic representation of classical ideas and culture had been propagated in northern Europe in the second half of the sixteenth century where the Italianate style found expression in architecture, painting, sculpture and prints, including maps. Knowledge of the ancient classics, the quintessential hallmark of the 'Renaissance' man, was reimagined though the use of elements steeped in both classical and Christian iconography. For example, the abstract concepts of 'constancy', 'patience', 'intellect' and 'truth' are incorporated as allegorical figures on the map where they act as supporters to the coats of arms of Ireland and Scotland. Though presented in the guise of a neoclassical vocabulary, the use of these devices is reimagined and aligned with Christian principles.

The Christian reference point is signalled in the treatment of the composition above the *Elenchus* compartment (see **3**), while the classical disposition is highlighted in the imagery used for that above the *Synopsis* (see **4**). Underpinning both presentations is the unspoken doctrine of the divine right of kings. God remains the heavenly king *in aeternum* and the power of earthly kings stems from him. Here the symbolism has been skilfully handled to highlight the legitimacy of Charles II as having a divine sanction for kingship, one that was

INTRODUCTION

not obtained by contract, actual or implied, between sovereign and people as argued by supporters of the former parliament during the English civil wars.[52] This exaltation of Charles II was clearly intentional in that the map imagery and text together declare the triumph of the Stuart dynasty while, at the same time, conveying the message that loyalty to a Catholic identity and a Protestant king were not incompatible.[53] It may be suggested that the opportunity of dedicating the map to the restored monarch, though operating within a conventional vocabulary of deference and patronage, was a significant motivating factor in its production.

THE ORIGIN OF THE MAP

The principal claims relating to the origin of the pictorial map were definitively set out by Hardiman in his *History*:

> In the year 1651 the Marquis of Clanricarde, then Lord Deputy of the kingdom, entered into a treaty with the Duke of Lorrain, to obtain twenty thousand pounds for the King's service in Ireland; for this sum, he agreed to give the City of Limerick and town of Galway as security; and directed his Commissioners, Lord Viscount Taaffe, Sir Nicholas Plunket and Geoffry Browne, Esquire, 'particularly to describe unto the Duke, the value of the security, the strength and situation of the places and the goodness and conveniency of the harbours, &c.' for this purpose, a map of the town was made, which, after the restoration, (when the antient inhabitants were restored, by the Crown, to their freedoms and estates,) was finished blazoned and described by the Rev. Henry Joyce, then warden;[54] and afterwards elegantly engraved, at the expense of the Corporation, and dedicated to King Charles II.[55]

The evidence adduced by Hardiman in support of the claim that it was made in 1651 to show the duke of Lorraine the situation and extent of the town cannot be substantiated. It is important to note that there is no reference to a map as such in the Lorraine proceedings recorded in *The memoirs and letters of Ulick, marquis of Clanricarde* (1757) or in de Burgo's *Supplementum* (1772), the two works referenced by Hardiman in this connection. Furthermore, the only two known early sources that have been interpreted as directly referring to this map (dated 1684 and 1709; see p. 4) make no mention of the Lorraine connection. In addition, one may question as to why Galway was singled out for special treatment. There is no similar map of Limerick, a town of no less importance at this period. Both Galway and Limerick are invariably mentioned together in the proceedings but only in the context of acting as security for the duke's loan. The considerable intrigue involved in these negotiations and the limited time available make it highly improbable that a map of this scale and detail could have been drawn up for the commissioners to take with them.[56] It seems evident that the statement made by Hardiman was an inference based on the following circumstantial evidence: firstly, a map would be a valuable addition to and illustration of their description of the town; second, one of the two surviving copies was in the possession of the descendants of Geoffrey Browne, one of Clanricard's three commissioners; and third (as outlined above) the map was intended to be accompanied by a descriptive work.[57]

Hardiman's other claim – that the map was 'elegantly engraved at the expense of the Corporation' – is equally open to question. If by 'corporation' he was referencing the new Protestant settlers in Galway who controlled civic affairs, it is inconceivable that these would have provided any assistance whatsoever towards this project.[58] It is unthinkable that those who had been installed as the new regime would in any way support the former inhabitants who were attempting to supplant their newly acquired wealth and status.[59] Rather, one must infer that Hardiman is here using it as a collective term for the former Catholic inhabitants who continued the 'corporation' in name for the purposes of electing their own warden and vicars.

The drawing of the map and the compilation of the various pieces of information contained in it must have taken some time. How long, is impossible to say, but inasmuch as it was planned to be accompanied by a descriptive memoir one may infer that supporting material already had been gathered by way of preparation.[60] Certainly, the level of detail depicted could not have been replicated from memory alone and must at some stage – probably at its initial compilation – been subject to a process of ground-truthing: regrettably, the names of the artist, engraver and printing house are unknown.[61] It seems likely that this project was in gestation for a number of years and was initiated in Galway. Hardiman appears to have come to this conclusion also and determined that the Lorraine negotiations offered the appropriate context to explain its origin.

It is difficult to move beyond conjecture in setting out the reasons behind the ultimate execution of this work. But it is likely that these are intimately bound up with the attempts by the Galway townsmen to recover the estates and properties confiscated by the Commonwealth. These landowners had lost much despite the assurances given in the articles of surrender in 1652.[62] Their hopes, however, had been raised by Charles II's initial attempt at grappling with the consequences of the land issue, his *Gracious Declaration* of 30 November 1660.[63] The former inhabitants were further flattered by the king in two letters sent to the lords justices towards the middle of the following year in which he acknowledged their loyalty and especially their defence of the town during its nine-month siege. In particular, he confirmed them 'to enjoy their respective freedoms, &c, houses and estates' under the articles of surrender and declared that he 'shall grant them such additional favours as they may claim under the terms of the peace of 1648. As we hear that some of the inhabitants especially deserve our favour you shall find out who they are and treat them as if they had been specially mentioned for good treatment in our declaration.'[64] Encouraged by the positive tenor of these sentiments, the former inhabitants presented a petition to the Irish privy council on 18 July 1661 requesting the immediate implementation of the king's letters. Having considered the matter the council, characteristically holding back from making a decision that would have had widespread implications, referred the petition back to him.[65]

The king, at his time, was being lobbied intensively by both Protestant and Catholic interests, each eager to convince him of the righteousness of their case. As has already been indicated, the former 'auld and auncient freemen' of Galway had established a special committee for this purpose.[66]   It was known that the king was a map enthusiast and not beyond being impressed by generous gifts. Working within the realm of courtly diplomacy, this map would be presented to him in much the same way as the monumental Klencke atlas had been in 1660, when a consortium of Dutch sugar merchants, led by Johannes Klencke, hoped that it might secure

them favourable trading privileges.[67] In the case of the Galway agents lobbying at court, what better way to prompt royal attention when making a submission than through the use of visual media, one that not only condensed the narrative of supplication but, in a very graphic way, encapsulated the 'supplication' in its entirety. In particular, the inclusion of the lines of the Cromwellian blockade (*Obsidionis Crumvelistae liniamenta*; see **27**) and the Cromwellian ships pursuing the king's subjects (*Crumvelistae naves persequentes Regis subditos*; see **38**) functioned as holdfasts that referenced the town's support for the Royalist cause. These images, together with the vivid declarations of loyalty to the king, would serve to remind him of his pledge to its mayor and corporation in February 1650 that he would 'in due time confer such privileges and favour upon you as may be lasting monuments of . . . our particular grace and acceptation thereof'.[68] Whether the king ever saw this map or was presented with a copy is not known: there is no evidence to suggest it. In the end, the Protestant argument won the day and in the words of a former Galway townsman, writing in 1661, those 'that had most money and best friends in court carried the game, and the poor Irish being utterly beggared attending to no purpose, sold their decrees to the English . . . by which means and other like courses and debentures of soldiers, the English invested themselves with all the estates in the county'.[69]

If, as is suggested, the production of this map was intended to play a supporting role in the real-life drama of those who were seeking influence at court for a return of their former estates and property,[70] then the likelihood is that it was printed shortly after Charles II's restoration. An indicative *terminus post quem* for the printing can be inferred from the inclusion on it of a shield on the top border labelled 'the arms of Guinea and Tangier'. Tangier, a major commercial centre on the north-west coast of Africa, was acquired by Charles II under the marriage contract with the *infanta*, Catherine of Braganza, of Portugal, signed on 23 June 1661. Although the marriage did not take place until June of the following year, court observers and others would have been aware of these newly acquired overseas possessions. It may be postulated that the map was printed either at the time that Catholics were lobbying at court as the new bill of settlement was being finalised in the Irish parliament in the second half of 1661 or, more likely, around the time of, or just after, the passing of the Act of Settlement in 1662. This was a fractious period when both Catholic

INTRODUCTION

and Protestant political contacts resumed their efforts at Whitehall to limit each other's perceived rights or, at the very least, gain some advantage for themselves and their patrons.[71] But this suggested date is simply a proposition based on an inference from the map's content. Future research may yet provide a more accurate account of its production and the motivation that prompted its compilation.

***

Given the map's socially determined and decidedly Catholic mental idealisation of the town and its environs, one of the most difficult tasks confronting the modern investigator is the determination of the level of trust that should be placed in it as a representation of Galway's physical landscape in the mid-seventeenth century. The map is not only of its genre and time, but has been larded through with additional levels of meaning by its compilers. To appreciate fully its geographical inclusivity it is necessary to strip out the schematic and conventional forms of picture-perfect representations, text, heraldic and other embellishments. When this has been achieved an extensive landscape is revealed, one that is bounded by the Terryland River on the north, the lands of Moneenagisha and the inner reaches of Lough Athalia on the east, Hare and Mutton Islands on the south and from Whitestrand to the immediate hinterland of Nun's Island on the west. As has been highlighted already (see above, p. 4), the decision to include considerable topographical detail outside the walled town within the confines of the printed map area has resulted in the distortion of their relative geographies. Considerable manipulation is required to align them with modern maps (see especially **34**).[72] Nonetheless, the inclusion of these features serves as a signpost to their perceived importance in presenting the town within its tangible and physical environment. It is at the micro level that the viewer's expectations of representational verisimilitude are intensified, at least, with regard to the more important public buildings and the town houses of named individuals. This is borne out, to an extent at least, by the portrayal of particular structures such as Ceann an Bhalla (see **10**), the Red Earl's Hall (see **13**), the new tholsel (see **15**) and St Nicholas's Church (see **22**). But there are indicators in the presentation of other elements that call for caution. The compilers' obvious desire to achieve representational perfection has, at times, distorted the appearance of certain features (see **10**, **11**, **27**, **34**, **35**). Yet the detailing of individual buildings and the layout of the streets and lanes testifies to a level of accuracy that must have been grounded in the real world.[73] While the modern viewer is faced with the dilemma of attempting to separate the 'real' from its 'representation', this predicament would not have troubled those members of Galway's former elite who purchased copies of the map. Sharing a collective perspective they would have accepted its relative accuracy and the quality of its engraving[74] as self-evident, and any infelicities or errors more than compensated for by the graphic hyperbole of its presentation.

For all its stylistic conventions and cartographical repetitions, the map provides a window into the culture and mindset of Galway's mid-seventeenth-century ruling Catholic elite. It is a glorification of their past, a map of things remembered, drawn up to ensure the commemoration of certain families and events. Most of all, it was intended to secure the survival of the town and its inhabitants into the future. It is very much part of the art of memory, a vibrant constituent of Renaissance intellectual culture that served to reinforce the status quo by drawing attention to its achievements. And for an exile such as Fr Henry Joyce, the map represented his home, his faith, his church, his haven of permanence and the cradle of security, peace and prosperity.[75] In this manner it acts as a symbolic mechanism that allows the empathetic viewer to transpose themselves back into another world. But this 'other' world was no longer in existence at the time of the map's printing. It must surely have been apparent to those responsible for its composition that the town was no longer in such a pristine, idyllic state.[76]

The viewer should not forget that this idealised portrait is the graphic testament of an ambitious and self-interested elite who, comforted by their shared religious conviction, sought to regain the wealth and status they had once enjoyed.[77] This is not to lessen the considerable achievement involved in the map's production for it offers an intimate insight into their hierarchies and values, into the hopes and desires of a generation that had experienced the annihilation of their world. More than anything else, it provides the modern viewer with the opportunity to inhabit this world. It is hoped that this book will equip the reader better to understand and appreciate the town that this map's creators historically delineated, that is, Renaissance Galway.

INTRODUCTION

[1] This map was formerly at Castlemagarret, Claremorris, Co. Mayo, and was presented to Queen's College Galway (now NUI Galway) in 1852 by Lord Oranmore; NUI Galway, Council Minute Book 1850–6, p. 140; James Mitchell, 'Mayor Lynch of Galway' in *JGAHS*, xxxii (1966–71), p. 54. There is every reason to believe that the presentation was instigated by the historian of Galway, James Hardiman, who was then (1852) librarian at the college; Marie Boran, 'James Hardiman, 1782–1855: the historian of Galway' in Próinséas Ní Chatháin, Siobhán Fitzpatrick with Howard Clarke (eds), *Pathfinders to the past: the antiquarian road to Irish historical writing, 1640–1960* (Dublin, 2012), p. 41. Hely Dutton, writing in the early 1820s, records that 'it would be highly desirous to have it copied, as it had a narrow escape from the flames when the house was consumed in 1812 [*recte* 1811]': *A statistical and agricultural survey of the county of Galway, with observations on the means of improvement; drawn up for the consideration, and by the direction of the Royal Dublin Society* (Dublin, 1824), p. 510.

The map was conserved at Trinity College, Dublin, *c.* 1988–1991, when it was found to have been backed with a number of first-edition Ordnance Survey 6-inch sheets. It is very likely that this was done in the mid-nineteenth century after it came into the possession of the college, before being framed behind glass and hung in the original library in the Quadrangle building. It was moved to the new library in 1973 where it was rehung off the foyer. In 1984 it was taken down by the librarian, Alf Mac Lochlainn, with a view to having it conserved. During the conservation process the secondary map backing was removed and the original map sheets separated and placed within archival polyester pockets: it is now housed in the Special Collections section of the James Hardiman Library. I am grateful to Timothy Collins, former chartered librarian at NUI Galway, and John Gillis, Conservation Department, Trinity College Library, for providing information on its conservation. A digital copy of this map is available on line at http://archives.library.nuigalway.ie/citymap/map.html; see Fergus Fahey, 'Italian echoes in the city of the tribes: pictorial map of Galway City' in *History Ireland*, xxi (2013), pp 18–19.

[2] It is not known when this copy came into the possession of Trinity College, Dublin, but it was discovered in its collections some time before 1816. On 9 January of that year the map was laid on fabric by George Mullen, who also made the case in which it has been thereafter kept folded along the sheet lines (https://digitalcollections.tcd.ie/home/index.php?DRIS_ID=MS1209_195, accessed 29 April 2018). That it had only recently been found among the library's collections may be inferred from a statement in James Hardiman's *History of the town and county of the town of Galway* (Dublin, 1820) where, in the prefatory postscript concerning the engravings, he records that the 'only copy, until lately . . . was preserved at Castlemagarrett . . . . In the meantime, a duplicate was discovered in the valuable library of Trinity College': *History*, p. x. William Wilde, writing in 1841, suggested that this copy was the one purchased by Molyneux in Galway in 1709: 'Sir Thomas Molyneux, Bart.' in *Dublin University Magazine*,

xviii (1841), p. 478; Mitchell, 'Mayor Lynch', p. 53, note 163. A digital copy of this map is available on line at http://digitalcollections.tcd.ie/home/index.php?DRIS_ID=MS1209_195.

A photolithographic reproduction of this copy was printed on a reduced scale by the Galway Archaeological and Historical Society in 1904 and a series of articles on the map were published in its journal: M.J. Blake, Caesar Litton Falkiner and W.F. Trench, 'Notes on the pictorial map of Galway' in *JGAHS*, iv (1905–6), pp 41–8; John McErlean, 'Notes on the pictorial map of Galway: the index to the map' in *JGAHS*, iv (1905–6), pp 133–60; E.C.R. Armstrong, 'The shields in the seventeenth-century map of Galway prepared for submission to the duke of Lorraine' in *JGAHS*, viii (1913–14), pp 235–6.

[3] Although a description of the map and its contents was given by Hardiman, it should be noted that there are some omissions and errors in the transcriptions provided there: *History*, pp 24–30.

[4] Examples of wall maps used in paintings of the Dutch golden age are best known through the paintings of Willem Buytewech (d. 1624), Quiringh van Brekelenkam (d. 1668), Johannes Vermeer (d. 1675) and Pieter de Hooch (d. 1684). They appear in almost a quarter of Vermeer's works and his 'The soldier and a laughing girl' (*c.* 1657), and 'The art of painting' (*c.* 1666–8) and van Brekelenkam's 'A family in an interior' (*c.* 1655) provide contemporary representations as to how such maps were hung: see James A. Welu 'Vermeer: his cartographic sources' in *The Art Bulletin*, lvii, no. 4 (Dec. 1975), pp 529–47; 'The map in Vermeer's *Art of Painting*' in *Imago Mundi*, xxx (1978), pp 9–30; Günter Schilder, *Monumenta cartographica Neerlandica VI. Dutch folio-sized single sheet maps with decorative borders, 1604–60* (Amsterdam, 2000), pp 47–8. The batons or rollers that were used to hang these maps invariably are depicted with intricately turned finials. These served not only as decorative embellishments but also had a practical function in keeping the map from contact with the wall, thus allowing air to circulate and protect it from damp.

[5] Such was the fate of the copy at St Isidore's which, in 1796, had not been cared for and was whitewashed in places: Edward MacLysaght (ed.), 'Report on documents relating to the wardenship of Galway' in *Analecta Hibernica*, no. 14 (1944), p. 72.

[6] The holes are best preserved along the top border and a number show rust staining from the iron tacks (see Fig. 1). The holes average *c.* 65mm apart. Nine of the estimated ten holes survive on the central top sheet, which suggests that some thirty tacks were used to fasten it to the top roller. Very little of the bottom map edge survives though a number of holes are visible.

[7] Wall maps were sometimes exported abroad as separate sheets which the purchaser could then have assembled at their destination. This was undertaken either for convenience or to save money, as noted *c.* 1570 by the great cartographer, Geraldus Mercator, in his instructions for their assembly. He recommended a glue composed of 'an application of wheat flour or spelt and boiled water': Cornelis Koeman, Günter Schilder, Marco van Egmond and Peter van der Krogt, 'Commercial cartography and map production in the Low Countries, 1500–*ca.*1672' in David Woodward (ed.), *History of cartography,*

INTRODUCTION

volume three: cartography in the European Renaissance (Chicago, 2007), pt 2, p. 1343.

[8] This may explain the presence of the surviving copy in the James Hardiman Library which came from Castlemagarret, Co. Mayo, the ancestral home of the Brown family of Galway.

[9] For John Speed's 'Invasions map' (1603–4), see Peter Barber, 'Mapmaking in England, *ca.* 1470–1650' in Woodward, *History of cartography, volume three,* pt 2, p. 1660, fig. 54.21. The frontispiece and county maps of Cambridgeshire, Oxfordshire and Suffolk in Speed's *The theatre of the empire of Great Britaine: presenting an exact geography of the kingdoms of England, Scotland, Ireland . . .* (London, 1611 [1612]) are noteworthy in being bordered with heraldic devices. By the middle of the seventeenth century, however, the inclusion of coats of arms on map borders became less common as the dictates of fashion demanded that these be decorated with town plans, portraits and topographical views, often combined with costumed figures of natives characteristic of the map area: Schilder, *Monumenta cartographica Neerlandica VI,* pp 55–81.

[10] Speed, *Theatre,* inset map following p. 143. This perspective was also used for the manuscript plan drawn in 1625 (TCD, Hardiman MS 1209/72), though it is most unlikely that the compilers of the Galway map would have had access to this. A similar perspective is to be found on Browne's outline plan of Galway, dated 1583: TNA:PRO, MPF 1/233. A comparable, though more elevated, view was chosen by Anthony Blake for his maps of the Galway fortifications *c.* 1755 (BL, Maps K Top 53 38 a, b, c). Perhaps he was influenced by a copy that he saw hanging in one of the Galway houses. For these maps, see Jacinta Prunty and Paul Walsh, *Galway/Gaillimh.* Irish Historic Towns Atlas, no. 28 (Dublin, 2016), map nos 7, 11, 20.

[11] For the origins and discussion of the bird's-eye perspective, see Lucia Nuti, 'The perspective plan in the sixteenth century: the invention of a representational language' in *Art Bulletin,* lxxvi (1994), pp 105–28; Hilary Ballon and David Friedman, 'Portraying the city in early modern Europe: measurement, representation, and planning' in Woodward, *History of cartography, volume three,* pt 1, pp 687–96. See also J.H. Andrews, *Maps in those days: cartographic methods before 1850* (Dublin, 2009), pp 64–71.

[12] By the late 1630s the Galway merchants were among the principal landowners in Connacht. In 1641 over 220,000 plantation acres of Connacht land were owned by Galway townsmen, of which almost 80,000 acres of profitable land were held by just twenty-five individuals: Brendán Ó Bric, 'Landholding by Galway townsmen in Connacht, 1585–1641' in *Irish Economic and Social History,* ii (1975), pp 60–1. For the context and mechanisms by which this was achieved, see Nicholas Canny, 'Galway: from the reformation to the penal laws' in Diarmuid Ó Cearbhaill (ed.), *Galway town and gown, 1484–1984* (Dublin, 1984), pp 20–4 and Raymond Gillespie, *Seventeenth-century Ireland: making Ireland modern* (Dublin, 2006), pp 112–13.

[13] For an analysis of the membership of the town council in the first half of the seventeenth century, see Bríd McGrath, 'Managing the Windsor of Ireland: the composition of Galway's town council, 1603–1653' in *JGAHS,* lxix (2017), pp 61–81. Seven Galway townsmen were returned as members of the

Irish parliament in 1634: Sir Valentine Blake (1st baronet, Galway), Nicholas Lynch (alderman, Galway), Sir Henry Lynch (1st baronet, Galway county), Sir Valentine Blake (junior, Tuam), Richard Oge Martin (Athenry), Dominick Brown (Athenry) and Patrick Darcy (Navan): Hugh Kearney, *Strafford in Ireland* (Manchester, 1959), pp 227, 247.

[14] Sir Valentine Blake, Baronet (*Elenchus,* W); Sir Richard Blake, Knight (*Elenchus,* Y); Sir Walter Blake, Knight (*Elenchus,* b); Sir Robert Lynch, Baronet (*Elenchus,* V); Sir Dominick Brown, Knight (*Elenchus,* Z); Sir Oliver French, Knight (*Elenchus,* &) and Sir Peter French, Knight (*Elenchus,* X).

[15] Noted Galway ecclesiastical luminaries at this time include Francis Kirwan (d. 1661), bishop of Killala, Andrew Lynch (d. 1681), bishop of Kilfenora, and Walter Lynch (d. 1663), bishop of Clonfert, who was warden at St Nicholas's College, Galway, before his elevation. At this period many sons and daughters of the nobility and merchant classes turned their backs on worldly careers and comfortable living and entered religious life or joined the priesthood: see F.X. Martin, '"So manie in the verie prime and spring of their youth, manie of them heirs of land": the friars of the Irish Capuchin mission in northern France and the Low Countries, 1591–1641' in Barbara Hayley and Christopher Murray (eds), *Ireland and France, a bountiful friendship: literature, history, and ideas. Essays in honor of Patrick Rafroidi* (Maryland, 1992), p. 15.

[16] Among the lawyers prominent in Galway affairs in the 1640s and 1650s may be mentioned Sir Richard Blake (d. 1663), Sir Valentine Blake (d. 1652), Geoffrey Browne (d. 1668), Patrick Darcy (d. 1668), Sir Henry Lynch (d. 1635), Sir Robert (Robuck) Lynch (d. 1667) and Richard Martin (d. *c.* 1659). All had trained at the Inns of Court, London: see Bríd McGrath, 'Ireland and the third university: attendance at the Inns of Court, 1603–1650' in David Edwards (ed.), *Regions and rulers in Ireland, 1100–1650* (Dublin, 2004), pp 217–36.

[17] The list constitutes a veritable who's who of the great families of Ireland. These are numbered on the map and have been identified as follows: on the left, (1) O'Brien, (2) O'Neill, (3) O'Reilly, (4) Clanrickard Burke, (5) Butler, (6) FitzGerald (Desmond), (7) Lynch (Knock, Co. Meath), (8) de Lacy, (9) Blake, (10) O'Driscoll (?), (11) Butler and (12) an ancient Burke arms; on the right, (13) Campbell (Argyll), (14) Blank, (15) Morris, (16) Burke (Lord Dunkellin?), (17) Cusack, (18) Butler, (19) O'Shaughnessy, (20) Bermingham, (21) Barrymore, (22) O'Reilly quartering O'Malley, (23) Martin impaling White and (24) Foster (?): Armstrong, 'The shields in the seventeenth-century map of Galway', pp 234–6.

[18] There is little doubt that many of the richer and better educated townspeople could converse in Latin. The papal nuncio, Rinuccini, who knew no English, preached several sermons in Latin during the two periods that he stayed in Galway and it is very likely that many in the congregation were capable of understanding them. Sir Richard Blake, a prominent Galway lawyer and Speaker of the Assembly of the Irish Confederation (see **6**), not only wrote and spoke Latin but also penned various verses in it. In 1647 he exchanged compliments with the nuncio in Latin verse on the occasion of the latter's visit to his suburban residence at Terryland. He also wrote, and had printed, a series of verses celebrating the Ormond peace: Stanislaus Kavanagh (ed.), *Commentarius Rinuccinianus de*

INTRODUCTION

sedis apostolicae legatione ad foederatos Hiberniae Catholicos per annos 1645–1649 (Dublin, 1932–49), ii, 678; iv, 33–7. As Sean O'Riordan has noted, 'Many, however, who would not trust themselves to write Latin probably spoke it quite fluently, if ungrammatically, and more again would understand it when spoken': 'Rinuccinni in Galway, 1647–49' in *JGAHS*, xxiii (1948–9), pp 32, 45.

[19] An interesting example is the name *P[latea] luti. Pludd streete* (*Elenchus*, 62). The name 'Pludd' undoubtedly is a transferred word from the Irish 'Pluda' or 'Plodach'. It can be suggested that the form Sráid Pluid (or perhaps Sráid Phluid), meaning 'muddy street', would have been in use in seventeenth-century Galway (pers. comm., Nollaig Ó Muraíle). It is of interest to note that the Latin, *lutum* means earth or clay, which could be interpreted as indicating that this street was unpaved. However, inasmuch as the cattle market (*Elenchus*, o) was held here, the name might well reflect the condition of this area in its aftermath.

[20] It is evident that Irish was spoken by many of the townspeople as the following incident, recorded in the 1641 Depositions, bears testament. In March 1642 the ship *Elizabeth and Francis* came to Galway from France with a cargo that included powder, shot and arms. It was boarded by a party of Galway townsmen led by Dominick Kirwan, a merchant and factor, who intended taking the ship's ordnance and munitions into the town. In the ensuing fracas the ship's surgeon, Robert Rawlins, was wounded but his life was saved by Thomas Martin, a merchant, who was one of the party that had boarded the ship. Dominick Kirwan had lunged at Rawlins with a 'skeane' but was stopped by Martin. Rawlins relates that they conversed in Irish – which he did not understand – and Kirwan then desisted from his attack: TCD, MS 831, fos 160, 197.

[21] Quoted in Mitchell, 'Mayor Lynch', p. 53.

[22] Ibid.

[23] Aquilla Smith (ed.), 'Journey to Connaught, April, 1709' in *Miscellany of the Irish Archaeological Society*, i (1846), p. 173.

[24] Thomas de Burgo, *Supplementum Hiberniae Dominicanae, varia virorum generum complectens additamenta* (1772), pp 922–3. Thomas Burke was sent to Rome to study in 1723. He was then only 13 or 14 years old and took the habit of the Dominican order in the following year: James Quinn, 'Burke (de Burgo), Thomas' in James McGuire and James Quinn (eds), *Dictionary of Irish biography* (Cambridge, 2009), ii, p. 59. His use of the phrase *primo vidi* (when I first saw) would suggest that he consulted the map on more than one occasion. He clearly took copious notes although the verses quoted by him from along the bottom border are given in a different order from those on the original.

[25] See Mitchell, 'Mayor Lynch', p. 54.

[26] Fr Francis Bermingham, a native of Co. Galway, was vicar-general of the order of St Francis and resided at the Irish Franciscan house, St Isidore's, Rome, in the mid-1650s. He published a volume of Scotist theology in 1656: Benignus Millett, *The Irish Franciscans, 1681–1685* (Rome, 1964), p. 479 and passim.

[27] MacLysaght, 'Report on documents relating to the wardenship of Galway', p. 72. It is clear from further incidental references in the letter that the map being described is the pictorial map of Galway. Fr Bodkin subsequently was Catholic Warden of Galway from 1805 to 1812: Martin Coen, *The wardenship of Galway* (Galway, 1984), p. 201.

[28] James Kelly (ed.), *The letters of Lord Chief Baron Edward Willes to the earl of Warwick, 1757–62: an account of Ireland in the mid-eighteenth century* (Aberystwyth, 1990), p. 85. His statement that 'the Tholsel and County Hall being built on the place where it stood' clearly is an error, based on either information that he was given or, more likely, his lack of familiarity with the streetscape of Galway.

[29] Woodward, *History of cartography, volume three*, pt 2, pp 1346–7.

[30] The overall layout and the lettering, especially in the cartouches, do not appear to be the work of the Amsterdam engravers. I am grateful to Peter Van der Krogt, Special Collections, University of Amsterdam, for his comments in this regard.

[31] It was not published or printed by the famous publishing house in Antwerp, the Plantin Press (pers comm., Dr Dirk Imhof, Museum Plantin-Moretus, Antwerp). That it was engraved and printed in the Low Countries is attested by the inclusion of a character found in the Dutch language – the dieresis on the letter 'y' (ÿ). It is used only in the indices where 'y' is not employed as a reference letter but operates as a ligature for the diphthong sound, as in the second syllable of the surname Athy, or placename, Galway (e.g., *Synopsis, in occidentem*, 37: 'the baÿ of Galwaÿ'). In line with cartographical usage the term 'Low Countries' is used in this essay rather than 'Netherlands': see Cornelis Koeman and Marco van Egmond, 'Surveying and official mapping in the Low Countries, 1500–*ca.* 1670' in Woodward, *History of cartography, volume three*, pt 2, p. 1246.

[32] Hardiman, *History*, p. 23.

[33] Ibid. Hardiman appears to have interpreted the word 'pastor' to mean that Henry Joyce held the post of warden during the reign of Charles I (repeated on p. 254, note a): this is incorrect. The post of Catholic Warden was held by Patrick Lynch from 1647 until his death in 1660 at Nantes, France. Henry's brother, Gregory, was then appointed as warden: Coen, *Wardenship*, pp 19–20. Both Henry and Gregory Joyce were vicars of St Nicholas's Church: Kavanagh, *Commentarius Rinuccinianus*, iii, pp 335, 494, 498, 598; v, p. 19. Henry Joyce may be identified with the priest of the same name mentioned in documents, dated 1637 and 1643, relating to the wardenship of Galway: MacLysaght, 'Report on documents relating to the wardenship of Galway', pp 27, 30, 31, 35.

[34] Henry and Gregory Joyce are recorded as ministering in secret in Galway in 1654: Millett, *Irish Franciscans*, pp 325–6. Thomas de Burgo records that they went into exile with their brother; *Hibernia Dominicana* (Kilkenny, 1762), pp 439–40.

[35] Brendan Jennings, *Wild Geese in Spanish Flanders, 1582–1700* (Dublin, 1964), p. 415.

[36] The map is very much a Catholic document in terms of both its text and its geography where every opportunity has been taken to include buildings or features that resonate with this confessional position. Eleven biblical quotations are directly referenced or alluded to in the cartouches on the map and, apart from detailing the various parts and altars of St Nicholas's Church, the tables list sixteen residences of male and female religious in the town, seven altars used for the Corpus Christi procession and seven other locations of various ecclesiastical edifices outside the walls.

[37] A document drawn up by the Dominicans at their house in Louvain, dated 8 January 1659, records their indebtedness to Gregory, Henry and William Joyce

INTRODUCTION

who 'have begun to build, under the title of the Holy Cross, the church of the Irish friars of the Holy Order of Preachers, at Louvain; the first stone blessed by the said Henry, by raising the walls from the foundations, by supplying much of the materials, by most liberally paying the fees and wages to architects and workmen in the course of the work . . . have expended such a large sum of money on the said fabric, and firmly purpose to expend still more'. They completed this work in 1666: Ambrose Coleman, *The Irish Dominicans of the seventeenth century by Father John O'Heyne, O.P.* (Dundalk, 1902), pp 283–5. John Lynch's life of Bishop Francis Kirwan is dedicated to Gregory Joyce and he is specifically mentioned as financing its publication: C.P. Meehan (ed.), *The portrait of a pious bishop; or, the life and death of the Most Rev. Francis Kirwan, bishop of Killala* (Dublin, 1884), p. iii.

In 1665 Henry Joyce was appointed dean of the chapter of the church of St Ursmer, at Binche, in the south-west of present-day Belgium but resigned this post in favour of a chaplaincy: Mitchell, 'Mayor Lynch', p. 52. Together with his brother Gregory he was included in a list (*c.* 1668) of Connacht theologians considered suitable for appointment as bishops and is described there as 'Henry Joyce of Tuam diocese, formerly a most vigilant pastor in Ireland, afterwards vicar general of the English king's army in Belgium, under the king of Spain, and appointed dean of Binche, in Hainaut'. Both were included in a subsequent similar list (1671): Benignus Millett, 'Calendar of volume 1 (1625–68) of the collection *Scritture riferite nei congressi, Irlanda* in Propaganda archives' in *Collectanea Hibernica*, 6–7 (1963–4), pp 30, 109. Mitchell has suggested that he retained his connection with Galway as a 'Henry Joyes' is recorded as having been elected one of the vicars in 1688, 1689 and 1690: Mitchell, 'Mayor Lynch', p. 52. The fact that a substitute was appointed in his stead in 1688 'until the said Father Joyce comes to serve the cure himself' suggests that he was appointed *in absentia*. He died at Binche in 1697, aged 80: Mitchell, 'Mayor Lynch', p. 52; MacLysaght, 'Report on documents relating to the wardenship of Galway', pp 157–8; James Rabbitte (ed.), 'Galway Corporation MS C' in *JGAHS*, xiv (1928–9), p. 9. As a vicar at St Nicholas's College, Henry Joyce would have been intimately acquainted with the church and this may account for the extensive listing of its various parts and altars in the map's index (see **22**).

[38] Among the records of the Blake family is a receipt, dated 4 July 1660, for monies expended by a member of 'the comittie appointed by the auld and auncient freemen late of Gallway, … for the supplying of the Agents to be imployed to our sacred and gracious majestie, Charles the second': M.J. Blake, *Blake family records, ii, 1600–1700* (London, 1905), pp 84–5.

[39] The ten named individuals identified in the map index belonged to five families (Blake 3, Brown 2, Darcy 1, French 2 and Lynch 2). Notable omissions from this list are members of the Kirwan and Martin families: for example, Richard Martin (d. 1648) and Edmond Kirwan (d. 1659), who also were wealthy landowners and influential members of the town's governing elite. It is noteworthy that at the time that this map was printed six of the named individuals were deceased, but their importance – and by association their surviving wives and families – was such that they were included.

[40] Given the bird's-eye perspective employed it was necessary to show this gate, which was then the only entrance to the town on its east side, beside the Lion Tower Bastion rather than in its true position: see Paul Walsh, 'The town walls and fortifications' in Elizabeth FitzPatrick, Madeline O'Brien and Paul Walsh (eds), *Archaeological investigations in Galway city, 1987–1998* (Dublin, 2004), p. 325.

[41] In this regard the map operates as a visual allusion that was intended to have a performative effect. For a discussion of maps as cartographic images, see Christian Jacob, *The sovereign map: theoretical approaches in cartography throughout history* (Chicago, 2006), pp 269–75.

[42] The selection of the number 'fourteen' is unquestionably a doubling of the septenary, the grouping or division of elements into seven. Whether or not this was intentional cannot now be ascertained but given the manifold occurrences of this number in the bible and, most especially, in the Book of Revelations, where it is referenced over fifty times, it is reasonable to suggest that it was purposely chosen by the compilers. The septenary pattern has had innumerable applications throughout history and features extensively in myth, art, architecture and religion. For a summary outline of its uses and context, see J.E. Cirlot, *A dictionary of symbols* (New York, 1971), pp 283–5.

[43] These fourteen families are explicitly referenced in the line of text that runs along the inner border of the compartment referencing the contents of the volumes that were to accompany this map. The fourteen headings or 'words' are there designated as corresponding to the fourteen families who are described as founders and patrons of the town (see fig. 3, p. 7).

[44] This comparison is elevated to biblical proportions in the quotations contained in the two cartouches below the *Elenchus* and *Synopsis* where the combined text is taken from Psalm 121:3–4. In this instance, the author has substituted 'Galway' for 'Jerusalem' in the original: *Galvia quoe aedificatur, ut civitas cujus participatio ejus in idipsum. Illuc enim ascenderunt tribus, tribus Domini: testimonium Israël, ad confitendum nomini Domini* (Galway, which is built as a city, whose participation is together in itself. For thither did the tribes ascend, the tribes of our Lord: the testimony of Israel, to confess unto the name of our Lord).

[45] It is difficult not to come to the conclusion that the number of ships depicted in the area of Ceann an Bhalla (Spanish Arch) and at the quays – exactly fourteen – was selected intentionally (see **10**).

[46] This map is the only evidence for the existence of Agnes' Tower: *Elenchus*, 27. A certain liberal interpretation of the number is evident in the way that five additional un-numbered entries are included in order to bring the total number of town gates up to the required 'fourteen'. Nor was it possible to confine everything to this number for, despite indicating otherwise, there are fifteen entries in the list of fortifications, the extra entry being given the number 5ᵃ. Although it does not seem likely, considering the amount of detail included, it is possible that some items or places were omitted from within the walled town as their inclusion would have meant exceeding that special figure. For example, the pillory is not recorded on the map though there is little doubt that it existed at this time. Nor can one claim that it was excluded on the grounds of its being an

INTRODUCTION

object for punishment and therefore inappropriate to be shown on the map, for the town gallows are depicted and aptly described in the index as the place where 'justice is executed' (*Synopsis: in orientem*, 40).

[47] The caduceus is typically associated with Mercury, the Roman god of messages, abundance and trade. As the messenger of the gods, he is usually represented as wearing winged sandals or a winged cap. For the Romans the caduceus served as a symbol for moral equilibrium and in later times, because of its association with Mercury, it became recognized as a symbol of commerce; see Cirlot, *A dictionary of symbols*, pp 35–6, 207–8.

[48] The fact that not one of the twenty-three cartouches of the arms of the Old English families allied to those of Galway contains a family name would also support the suggestion that the map had not been finished at the time of printing. In addition, one of the shields (no. 14) on the right-hand border together with those of the king's American, West Indian and African dominions are blank. One is left with the impression that the requirement of having it available by a particular date was the determining factor in bringing it to press.

[49] The king is depicted wearing a crown and garter sash and is clad in armour. There is a marked similarity between this representation and the commemorative engraving of Charles II produced in 1660 which, ironically, was a reworking of a portrait of Oliver Cromwell; see www.royalcollection.org.uk/collection/themes/exhibitions/charles-ii-art-power/the-queens-gallery-buckingham-palace/charles-ii-3 (accessed 18 March 2018).

[50] On the left are the arms of England, Scotland, Wales and France; in the centre are the arms of the five Irish provinces (Munster, Connacht, Meath, Leinster and Ulster) and the blank shields to the right are identified as belonging to the colonies in America, the West Indies and Africa.

[51] The extended phrase *non plus ultra* may be translated as: '(Let there) not (be) more (sailing) beyond' a warning to mariners that these marked the end of known classical world. The earliest recorded use of the later Latin version *ne plus ultra*, meaning '(go) no more beyond', in English dates to 1638: *The Oxford English dictionary* (2nd ed. Oxford, 1989), x, p. 326. The pillars and inscribed ribbons were first used as part of the armorial bearings of Charles I (1500–58) of Spain, who was also Holy Roman Emperor, Charles V, and they continue to be part of the modern coat of arms of that country.

[52] The historian and polemicist, Fr John Lynch (d. 1677), a contemporary townsman, expressed similar laudatory sentiments in his introductory epistle of *Cambrensis eversus* (published 1662). The epistle, which is dedicated to Charles II, incorporates numerous quotations from the bible, church fathers and classical writers in support of his plea to have the Irish restored to their estates and properties: Matthew Kelly (ed.), *Cambrensis eversus* (3 vols, Dublin, 1848), i, pp 3–79.

[53] In this regard, the map may be making an oblique contribution to contemporary political debate within the Irish Catholic Church which had been polarised as a result of the papal nuncio's interdict of 1648: see Anne Creighton, 'The Remonstrance of December 1661 and Catholic politics in Restoration Ireland' in *Irish Historical Studies*, xxxiv, no. 133 (May 2004), pp 16–41.

[54] As noted above, Henry Joyce did not hold the post of warden (see note 33).

[55] Hardiman, *History*, p. 23.

[56] The negotiations are set out in some detail in M.D. O'Sullivan, *Old Galway* (Cambridge, 1942), pp 287–326 and E.P. Duffy, 'Clanricarde and the duke of Lorraine' in *JGAHS*, xxxi (1964–5), pp 71–99.

[57] These misgivings were expressed by the editor (W.F. Trench) of the *Journal of the Galway Archaeological and Historical Society* where he spoke on behalf of his fellow authors, Martin J. Blake and Caesar Litton Falkiner; 'Notes on the pictorial map of Galway' in *JGAHS*, iv (1905–6), pp 42–3. Despite this rejection of the Lorraine connection, it continued to be cited as the reason for the map's compilation; e.g., O'Sullivan, *Old Galway*, p. 293; Duffy, 'Clanricarde and the duke of Lorraine', p. 83, note 69; Sean Spellissy, *The history of Galway* (Limerick, 1999), p. 59.

[58] Taking this statement at face value, R.C. Simington noted that the map might be seen as the reply made by the inhabitants on this occasion, suggesting it was 'not inconceivable that the ex-Puritan and pro-Restoration corporation considered it a good investment – a coat of arms-edged security – to pay under the counter, putting it crudely, for this attractive map'. *Books of survey and distribution: being abstracts of various surveys and instruments of title, 1636–1703, iii, County of Galway* (Dublin, 1962), p. lviii. This is most unlikely. The members of the Protestant corporation at Galway were far from being supporters of Charles II. Sir Charles Coote records that he had to imprison 'the mayor, one of the sheriffs and several of the inhabitants who (being fanatics)' refused to join with him in declaring for the king; *Cal. S.P. Ire. 1660–2*, p. 423. As W.F. Trench succinctly put it, 'That they took so manifest an interest in the history of the town as to be pleased at the prominence of certain ancient families all of whom they themselves in fact supplanted – is there *any* body of men that we can credit with such sublimely disinterested conduct?'; 'Notes on the pictorial map of Galway', p. 43.

[59] A demonstration of the contempt that the Protestant members of the Common Council had for the 'auld natives of Galway' is evinced in the abuse bestowed on Martin French, who, in February 1662, attempted to implement an order of the lords justices. He was 'cuffed about the head' by the wife of one of the Aldermen, Paul Dodd, his hat thrown in the gutter, he received two blows to his head from the sheriff, John Murray, and was stripped, searched and imprisoned for two hours before being released; *20th report of the deputy keeper of the public records in Ireland* (Dublin, 1888), app., pp 32–3.

[60] It is tempting to speculate that the 'book in folio, four fingers thick, a manuscript written in English . . . where they are wont to write the antiquities and most remarkable things that happened in the said town of Galway' formed the basis for part of the descriptive element of this work; James Hardiman, 'The pedigree of Doctor Domnick Lynch, Regent of the colledge of St Thomas of Acquin, in the city of Seville' in *Miscellany of the Irish Archaeological Society*, i (1846), pp 65–6. As this book was kept by the college at Galway it is likely that it was known to Fr Joyce who was a vicar.

[61] Various changes were made to the plates during the engraving and proof stages; for example, the embankment for the mill-race to the south of the west bridge was added after this section of town wall had been engraved (see **11**). In certain instances substantial revisions were necessitated, as in the area of present-day Prospect Hill and the southern suburb (see **4**). Each of the four medallions on

INTRODUCTION

the top border is framed by an inscribed band. The inscription around one of these (second from right) contains an error which was picked up at proof stage and an asterisk was used to designate the missing word which is printed outside the frame (see fig. 4, p. 8).

[62] For the various attempts by the Galway townsmen throughout the 1650s and early years of Charles II's reign to retain the guarantees that they had secured under the terms of the articles of capitulation in 1652, see John Cunningham, *Conquest and land in Ireland: the transplantation to Connacht, 1649–1660* (Woodbridge, 2011), pp 57–63, 91–9, 121–30.

[63] *His majesties gracious declaration for the settlement of his kingdome of Ireland, and satisfaction of the several interests of adventurers, soldiers, and other his majesties subjects there*. This is incorporated within the Act of Settlement, 1662, 14 and 15 Car. II. c. 2; *Irish statutes: revised edition. 3 Edward II to the Union, A.D. 1310–1800* (London, 1885), pp 90–105. It was the eminent Galway lawyer Patrick Darcy who demonstrated that a royal declaration was not a sufficient basis for the determination of property rights and that an act of the Irish parliament would be needed: see Danielle McCormack, *The Stuart Restoration and the English in Ireland* (Woodbridge, 2016), p. 18.

[64] M.J. Blake (ed.), 'Galway Corporation Book B' in *JGAHS*, v (1907–8), pp 72–3; *Cal. S.P. Ire., 1660–2*, pp 356–7. See also Hardiman, *History*, pp 141–2. That these letters gave the former inhabitants high expectations of being restored to their properties and possessions is attested by the following incident. At the end of June or in early July 1661, Robert Martin of Ross came to Galway to do some business with the recorder, Edward Eyre, who had been granted Martin's former house in the town. Martin intimated to Eyre that the king's letter would allow him take possession of this property. Eyre responded that, as the letters had not been sealed by the lords justices, they were not worth 'threepence'. Martin subsequently accused him of an 'undervaluation of the king's authority' and, as such, Eyre had 'spoken treason'. The case ended up in the Irish House of Commons where Eyre, 'having received some handsome encomiums for his loyalty and integrity, was unanimously acquitted': Hardiman, *History*, pp 142–4; McCormack, *Stuart Restoration*, p. 75.

[65] Among the group of six citizens representing the interests of Galway and Limerick that presented the petition, four were prominent Galway townsmen: Sir Richard Blake, Patrick Darcy, Patrick Kirwan, and Nicholas French. In a meeting with the privy council on 18 July 1661, they informed the members that 'they expected to be restored to those cities and towns as they were before the rebellion', including their rights to be elected as magistrates etc. The response from the court at Whitehall, dated 12 August, noted that while certain clauses of the king's letter 'might have been more warily expressed', his majesty 'had no intention the grace and favor held forth by that letter should be extended further then to *innocent* papists' as set out in his Gracious Declaration: Peter Gale, *An inquiry into the ancient corporate system of Ireland* (London, 1834), app., pp cxxxii–cxli. The matter was considered again at the privy council in August 1663 and the council members, no doubt anxious to ensure an equitable outcome for

those favoured by the king, referred it back once more to the monarch: *Cal. S.P. Ire., 1663–5*, pp 195–6.

[66] See note 38.

[67] Franz Reitinger, 'Bribery not war' in Peter Barber (ed.), *The map book* (New York, 2005), pp 164–5. The Klencke atlas contains 41 copperplate wall maps constituting the greatest examples of Dutch cartography in the mid-seventeenth century: Tom Harper, 'The Klencke Atlas' at www.bl.uk/picturing-places/articles/the-klencke-atlas (accessed 23 April 2018) where the atlas contents are available on-line.

[68] J.T. Gilbert (ed.), 'Archives of the town of Galway' in *Historical Manuscripts Commission, tenth report*, app., pt v (London, 1885), pp 499–500.

[69] This account would appear to have been written by Geoffrey Lynch fitz Dominick in 1661: see Paul Walsh, 'Account of the town of Galway' in *JGAHS*, xliv (1992), pp 51–2, 76. While these remarks were expressed with reference to the proceedings of the Loughrea commissioners in the mid-1650s they are equally relevant as commentary on events at this time.

[70] Numerous efforts were made at this time by different Catholic interest groups working in Dublin and London to influence the king and many of the dispossessed Irish in exile on the Continent also were actively supporting this cause. For example, the Galway native, Fr John Lynch, in the dedicatory epistle (probably written in late 1661 or early 1662) to his *Cambrensis eversus* pleads with the monarch to re-establish the 'rightful lords . . . in their estates, and the inhabitants of cities in their former dwellings': *Cambrensis eversus*, i, p. 79.

[71] The act passed both houses of the Irish parliament in May 1662 and was given royal assent on 31 July: L.J. Arnold, *The restoration land settlement in county Dublin, 1660–1688* (Dublin, 1993), p. 47. For some Galway townspeople – Sir Richard Blake, Geoffrey Browne and the heirs of Sir Valentine Blake, in particular – this act would prove fortunate as their names were included with others who were to be restored 'forthwith' to their estates: Act of Settlement, 1662, 14 and 15 Car. II. c. 2, section ccxxv; *Irish statutes*, p. 175. For the efforts of Dame Elinor Blake and members of other Galway families in reclaiming their lands under the Act of Settlement, see *Blake family records*, ii, pp 88–97.

[72] See Paul Walsh, 'The topography of the town of Galway in the medieval and early modern periods' in Gerard Moran and Raymond Gillespie (eds), *Galway: history and society* (Dublin, 1996), pp 34–5 and fig. 2.2.

[73] The inclusion of detailing such as external stairs within a small number of courtyards, a timber walkway at first-floor level in another, the depiction of St John's Lane (*Elenchus*, 74) as running underneath four houses and the representation of houses with arcaded ground floors cannot but be considered as portraying real features and structures. That said, a comparison of the various house representations on the map with the limited surviving fabric suggests some element of generic schematisation in the treatment of their frontages. For example, the house facing Market Street (present Cooke's Restaurant) is of three bays but is depicted on the map with four. The building on the corner of Whitehall and Abbeygate Street Lower, though converted to a corn store in the

INTRODUCTION

nineteenth century, retains its original sixteenth-century corner and adjacent doorway at street level: this doorway is not depicted on the map.

[74] The engraving displays little of the masterly skill that was characteristic of maps published in the Low Countries during the sixteenth and seventeenth centuries: see Woodward, 'Techniques of map engraving, printing, and coloring in the European Renaissance' in Woodward, *History of cartography, volume three*, pt 2, pp 591–610. For examples of significant Dutch maps and charts published for the period 1550–1700, see Günter Schilder, *Monumenta cartographica Neerlandica* (9 vols, Amsterdam, 1986–2013). Although the compilers of the Galway map may have wished to aspire to the splendour of existing large-scale bird's-eye views such as those of Amsterdam (1625) by Balthasar Floriszoon van Berckenrode (reprinted with amendments in 1648 and 1657) or Madrid (1656) by Pedro Teixeira (engraved and published in the Low Countries), the finished product does not compare with the high-quality work displayed on these maps. While there is every reason to conclude that a single individual was responsible for engraving the pictorial map of Galway, the variation in the representation of the water in the bay area suggests that either the engraver was eager to complete this section of the map or was not concerned with stylistic uniformity (visible in **30** and **38**). It is possible that a second, and less assured hand, was drafted in to engrave this part of the map.

[75] In 1669 his fellow exiled townsman, Fr John Lynch, reminisced on his 'famed city of Galway, the metropolis of Connaught, which a short time ago could not exhibit a population so numerous, merchants so opulent, or wealth so flourishing. This city was adorned with green marble walls, flanked by numerous towers; within the precincts of these walls were edifices, for the most part four or five stories high, built of the same green marble: its noble squares and fair proportions, symmetrically elegant, gladdened the eye; so much so, that Galway has ever appeared to me, what Jerusalem was to Jeremias – a city of most perfect beauty': Meehan, *Portrait of a pious bishop*, pp 17–18.

[76] The ruination of the town under the Commonwealth administration is evinced from the account by Henry Cromwell who had visited Galway in 1656. Writing in April 1657, he noted that its 'many noble buildings, uniform, and most of them marble, which that country hath plenty of; yet by reason of the late horrid rebellion, and general waste then and since made by the impoverished English inhabiting there, many of the houses are become very ruinous': Thomas Birch (ed.), *A collection of the state papers of John Thurloe, volume VI, 1657–58* (London, 1742), pp 209–10. Immediately after the surrender of the town in 1652 two substantial citadels were built inside the main entrances at the east and west. The western or lower citadel, as it became known, was built on the site of Sir Richard Blake's town house (marked 'Y' on the map (*Elenchus*); for its location, see **11**) and the east or upper citadel blocked off all access to the Great Gate (see **8**). Both citadels are shown on Thomas Phillips's 1685 plan of Galway: NLI, MS 3137 (28); Prunty and Walsh, *Galway/Gaillimh*, map 13.

[77] This idealised view of Galway contrasts with the comments of a contemporary townsman, Geoffrey Lynch fitz Dominick, on the social and business mores of some of its merchant elite. Writing in 1661, he observed: 'You may suppose that these three ensuing things brought no good to this town of Galway but rather ambition, dishonour and discredit, to wit knights, lawyers and bomery [*recte* bottomry]-masters, discredit when all matters were formerly tried and indeed by two honest burgesses and friends, and the bomery [*recte* bottomry]-masters to the highest degree, when in old times they would rather hang themselves than break, or discontent strangers. Now it's made a common trade to deceive them to the greatest dishonour of the good and famous character evermore held of the town, and their true and honest dealings. Likewise the said town is infected with pride, none being capable of good marriage or portion however so well bred, or good conditioned or virtuous, except he had a stone house, or good estate, and likewise the sin of lechery did abound': Hardiman, *History*, p. 126, n. t.; Walsh, 'Account of Galway', p. 74.

INTRODUCTION

Part II ~ Map extracts and commentaries

The copy of the pictorial map used for the extracts is in the Manuscript and Archives department of the library in Trinity College, Dublin, and is reproduced with the permission of the Board of Trinity College. See the editorial note on p. viii for further details.

CAROLVS R

BERNIÆ CLARISSIMÆ METROPOLIS, ET EMPO

C R

9

Terra, fretū, populi, quæque aſpicis undique late
Sunt tibi, sint generi, Carole fida tuo .

L C f

Plus vltra tibi, quā tabulæ, vel continet Orbis.
Quæſphera ſuperāt, ſuſpice, noſce tua .

L C f

DIEV ET MON DROIT

AVGVSTISSIMO, FAVSTISSIMOQVE SVO PRINCIPI
CAROLO II. DEI Gᵃ ANGLIÆ, SCOTIÆ, FRANCᵉ & HIBERⁿᵉ REGI Serenissino, &c.
Ab adictiſſimo Suæ Mᵗⁱˢ chete R.D.H.I. istius Vrbis ciue, & paſtore oblata .
Ciuitatē, et ſe, ſuaq; omnia, in, et extra vrbē, D.Ö.M, & SSⁱ S.M. æterno voto Conſecrat, dedicatque
S P Q G.

14 G
Laudatio eius manet in ſæculū ſæculi

Caſula quam colimus Veſtra eſt, iam reſpice pictam
Nos quoque ſacramus noſtraque noſque tibi .

L F

Fig. 5: The 'most ancient' arms (left), the 'old' arms (middle) and a variation of the Galway arms used from the later seventeenth to the nineteenth centuries (right).

Three different coats of arms of Galway are displayed on the map. The town's principal arms are given prominence both in terms of size and placement; they are suspended with three chain-links from the cartouche containing the dedicatory inscription to Charles II indicating the town's position in the hierarchy of authority. The cartouches below each of the Galway arms contain couplets extolling the loyalty of the inhabitants to the king (see p. 9). The arms are recorded in the map index as *Galviae civitatis antiquissima* (12), *vetusta, &* (13ᶠ) *recentiora insignia* (14ᴳ) – the most ancient, the old and the more recent arms of Galway (*Synopsis: in orientem*). Above each shield is a line of text which, taken together, constitutes two verses from the Book of Psalms (Ps 110:10–11): *Initium sapientiæ timor Domini; intellectus bonus omnibus facientibus eum: laudatio ejus manet in sæculum sæculi* (The fear of our Lord is the beginning of wisdom; understanding is good to all that do it: his praise remaineth for ever and ever).

The shield containing the 'most ancient' arms was intended to display a quartering of the arms of de Burgh with those of the Mortimers, earls of March. The Mortimers claimed possession of the de Burgh estates in right of the marriage of Lionel Mortimer to Elizabeth, countess of Ulster, in 1352. The form of the arms depicted here, though undoubtedly harking back to those of Roger Mortimer (1374–98), are incorrectly rendered both in terms of the positioning of the ordinaries and the hatching used to indicate the tinctures. A version of the Mortimer arms was in use in Galway from the later fourteenth century until *c.* 1485. Although described here as the most ancient arms used by the town, this is not correct. The earliest arms used by town officials were those of its founders, the de Burghs.

The shield displaying the 'old' arms of the town contains a chevron and three triple-towered castles. Little is known about them and they appear to be derived from personal arms. It has been suggested that they are a version of the Lynch arms (a prominent wealthy Galway family) to which they bear some resemblance. They were used in the fifteenth century but did not supersede those of the Ulster-March arms as both appear to have been in simultaneous use.

The 'more recent' arms are those that are still used by the city and were granted to the town some time after 1578, possibly when its charter was renewed by Elizabeth I in 1580. They consist of a golden galley floating on waves and placed on a silver shield. Hanging from the single mast, which has furled sails, is a smaller shield (black) bearing the device of a golden lion. The galley clearly represents the town's maritime trading connections but the origin of the golden lion on the black shield is unknown. These arms can be seen on the west face of the Great Gate (see **8**) and are represented on the plaques that were set in the fortifications in the mid-seventeenth century (see **9**). The central design (the galley with a hanging shield) has remained constant, though in a number of instances the shield is shown not with the golden lion but with a version of the royal arms of England. This variant was used occasionally from the later seventeenth until the end of the nineteenth century and no satisfactory explanation for its occurrence has been found.

1. THE ARMS OF GALWAY

ATHEY BLAKE BODKIN BROWNE DEANE

L C F L C F L C F L C F L C F

DORSIE FONTE FRINCH IOYCE

L C F L C F L C F L C F

KIROWAN LINCH MARTINE MORECH SKERETH

L C F L C F L C F L C F L C F

Whether or not one accepts the theory that the label 'tribes' of Galway' was first used as a term of reproach by the Cromwellian soldiers, its origin would appear to lie in its adoption as a mark of distinction by the former Catholic ruling families in the aftermath of the Williamite wars. In order to preserve the separate Catholic wardenship – a quasi-independent ecclesiastical structure established in 1485 and empowering the local corporation to elect members of the collegiate church of St Nicholas – the old Galway families established an unofficial Catholic 'corporation'. Over time they seized exclusive control of its electoral machinery and by the second quarter of the eighteenth century were known as the 'tribes'. The other Catholic families who did not have voting rights were referred to as 'non-tribes', a matter that resulted in a number of disputes throughout the century. Nor was there always agreement on precisely how many families constituted the so-called 'tribes'. Some lists excluded either the Deane, Font or Morris families considering that their members did not play a particularly important role in the civic history of the town. The publication, in 1820, of the *History of Galway* by James Hardiman effectively settled the exact number as fourteen and the establishment of the Catholic diocese of Galway, in 1831, extinguished their quasi-official powers.

The earliest historical reference to the term 'tribes' is encountered on this map. It is included in the series of Latin verses underneath the armorial bearings of fourteen families along the bottom border whose names are listed as *Athey, Blake, Bodkin, Browne, Deane, Dorsie, Fonte, Frinch, Joyce, Kirowan, Linche, Martine, Morech* and *Skereth*. Most of these tribal families could claim by ancestry and prescription, arising from ancient custom, to trace their roots to the foundation of the town in the early thirteenth century. Many were of Anglo-Norman origin who, over time, admitted a small number of Gaelic families (e.g., members of the Ó Dorchaidh, anglicised D'Arcy or Darcy, and Ó Ciardubháin, anglicised Kirwan) into their ranks. Their descendants – especially those of the Blake, Brown, Darcy, French, Kirwan, Lynch and Martin families – became successful merchants and traders who contributed to establishing Galway as an integral and substantial factor in the mercantile life of the west of Ireland in the sixteenth and first half of the seventeenth century.

Among the most successful of these families were the Lynches, who could trace their presence in the town as far back as 1274 when a Thomas Lynch (or de Lince) was provost or chief magistrate. This family was a powerful force in the public life of the town. The first mayor of the town was a Lynch and between 1485 and 1654 – the year in which the last mayor elected by the old Galway families was deposed by the Cromwellian governor – over eighty members of that family held this office. Their distinguished contribution is reflected in the fact that the arms of four separate branches of this family are included on the bottom border of the map.

It is important to note, however, that the so-called 'tribes of Galway' did not possess legal authority or validity and were never given formal recognition in any grant or charter, despite their presumption of such in the local church politics of the eighteenth century. Many of these family names are still to be found in the city and its environs, though a number – Athy, Font and Skerrett – are largely extinct.

There are a small number of notable differences between the arms of the tribal families depicted on the map and their later equivalents. Of particular interest are those of the Darcy and Morris families. The arms of the latter, as depicted on the map, were probably in contemporary use though no example survives in Galway. They are markedly different to those that became established in later years and which are represented in Hardiman's *History of Galway* (1820). This is also the case with the Darcy arms, which may be seen on the surviving doorway, dated 1624 (see **21**). The modern, recognised Darcy arms (depicted in Hardiman's *History*) are those of D'Arcy of Platten, Co. Meath, which were misapplied to the Galway family in the mid-eighteenth century. It is also noteworthy that the tincture indicated by the hatching on the background of the Martin arms represents vert (green) rather than azure (blue), which is usually found. While some of the differences may reflect local variations others probably resulted from a lack of knowledge of the application of the rules of heraldry.

2. THE 'TRIBES' OF GALWAY

The allegorical compositions above the compartments containing the *Elenchus* and *Synopsis* reflect in their constituent elements a language of intercession, which was the common coin of contemporary discourse among the elites of Renaissance Europe. Both employ fictive motifs – the classically-inspired Palladian doorway – that act as presentational devices to articulate meanings and significances that go beyond the spoken or written word. The inclusion of such devices with sculpted figures was commonplace in the graphic media of Europe in the later sixteenth and first half of the seventeenth centuries where engravings and paintings embracing Christian and classical elements became popular among the elites, especially the urban intelligentsia.

In this sacral composition prominence is given to the reclining figure of God the Father who is appropriately positioned on top of the doorway at the centre of the broken curved pediment. In typical Renaissance fashion he is depicted here as a benign – though somewhat disinterested-looking – patriarch with white hair, a beard and the equilateral nimbus or halo signifying the Trinity. He holds the sceptre with the fleur-de-lis, symbolising his position as the divine ruler. Underneath his right arm is a wooden vessel from which flows a stream of water. This pose originates in classical antiquity and variations are used on the map for both the river and sea gods (visible in **5** and **10**). Here the reclining figure is Christianised, presenting God the Father as the font and origin of eternal life through the addition of an inscription that begins on the rim of the vessel and is continued below the figure, *Fons aquae salientis in vitam aeternam*. This derives from the gospel of St John where, at the meeting between Jesus and the Samaritan woman at the well, Jesus declared 'the water that I will give him, shall become in him a *fountain of water springing up unto life everlasting*' (John 4:13–14).

The divine link is further highlighted through the use of a series of winged *putti*. One reads a book (the Bible), another holds a sceptre and olive branch (right), symbols of imperial authority and Pax, the Roman goddess of peace. Two further *putti* – appropriately sad of countenance – sit on the plinth; one (left) holds a crown of thorns and a bulrush, referencing the mocking of Christ before his crucifixion, while the other (right) holds a lighted candle (torch) and sword with an ear attached at the centre, an iconographic pairing pointing to the capture of Jesus in the garden of Gethsemane when Simon Peter cut off the ear of the high priest's servant (John 18:10). Both angels stand on pedestals and carry the symbols of the passion: the cross, lance, vinegar-soaked sponge (right), pillar, nails and scourge (left). The little winged-head clasp and the cruder version on the buskin of the right-hand figure are stock motifs found in devotional art and prints, especially those depicting the archangel Michael.

With outstretched arms, the angels hold up a laurel wreath containing the words *ipsi honor & gloria in saecula*, a continuation of the inscription along the frieze directly above. Taken together they read: *In tuo omnia, aequo omnia, per tuem omnia. Ipsi honor & gloria in saecula*, a reference to St Paul's letter to the Romans (11:36) where he says: *Quoniam ex ipso et per ipsum et in ipso omnia ipsi gloria in saecula* (for of him, and by him, and in him are all things: to him be glory for ever).

The centre-piece of the composition, the roundel, is headed with the abbreviation D.O.M.S., *Deo Optimo Maximo Sacrum* (Sacred to God, Most Good, Most Great). This abbreviation gained currency during the Renaissance and was carved, usually contracted to D.O.M., on buildings and funerary monuments where it frequently prefaced an inscription. In this case it serves as the label for the index to the contents of the work referring to the letters that accompany the text and images on the map. Below the roundel the monogram D.IHS.C. – *Domine Jesu Christe* (Lord Jesus Christ) – is placed above the words *Sit nomen Domini benedictum in eternam* (The name of our Lord be blessed for ever), a blessing derived from the Book of Psalms (112:2) used in many Catholic liturgies. To reinforce the allegorical message, the composition sits above a double cartouche containing an appropriate quotation from Psalm 91:11 – *Angelis suis Deus mandavit de te, ut custodiant te in omnibus viis tuis* (God has given his angels charge of thee: that they keep thee in all thy ways).

3. A LANGUAGE OF DEFERENCE – THE CHRISTIAN DIMENSION

Hæc quoque
SS. R. M. D.

Vt superius Agnoscuntur & infra
+ Epistola dedicatoria
B Sui Principatus Excellentiæ Sign
    Arma
C Regionum
    Gentium
    Insignia
D Regnorum
    Nationum
    Scuta
E Diversarum Terrarum
    Populorum
    Angliæ Regis
F Monarchiæ

C. II. R.

Rex Carolus, magnus Monarcha viuet in ævum

IN MANIBVS POR-   NE FORTE OFFÊDAS
TABVNT TE   AD LAPIDÊ PEDÊ tuũ
        L C F   L C F

SYNOPSIS

The Renaissance notion of kingship embraced the idea that whereas the body politic was united with the king, the king was not united to the body politic: the king was a 'being' apart, a separate entity that transcended time. To intercede with the sovereign necessitated a special language of deference, a contemporary rhetoric that drew on both Christian – especially Catholic – and classical allegorical imagery to reinforce not only the message of supplication but the sovereign's position as the font and source of all favour. In this composition, which is devoted to highlighting the map elements connected to Charles II, classical connotations are palpable in the vibrant monumental scheme. The artist has incorporated two Roman deities to emphasise this aspect of the royal estate and the motifs employed epitomise everything that they epitomised for the ancients: Charles II is, by association and support, on a par with the classical pantheon.

A debased form of Palladian-inspired doorway frames the upper part of the composition where the royal arms of Charles II are fittingly positioned at the centre of the broken pediment. And to accentuate the classical theme, Roman oil lamps burn at either end of the pediment. Below this and supported by draped garlands is a roundel referencing in abbreviation his most serene highness, *C[arolus] II, R[ex]*, and containing an index to the various items on the map that relate to the king and his dominions (lettered B–F on the top border).

The Roman gods are represented as terminal figures in the manner of caryatids (carved pillars in female form used to support the entablature of a classical building) except that here the figures are out of proportion to the doorway they flank, detracting from their architectural purpose. To the right, the helmeted figure of Minerva, the goddess of wisdom, science, war and arts, carries the Aegis, the divine shield with the head of Medusa across it with which to strike terror in her enemies. On the left, the laurelled figure of Apollo holds the lyre and a sunburst emblem, reflecting his association as the god of music and his personification as the Greek sun god Helios. The deities stand on either end of a cartouche declaring: *Rex Carolus Magnus Monarcha vivat in aevum* (May King Charles, the great monarch, live forever). The symbolism employed is powerful and explicit in its message: the king has triumphed over his enemies (Minerva) and the dawn of a new era has arrived (Apollo).

The link between this composition and the compartment below is effected by a cartouche that, mirroring that in the same position above the *Elenchus* table (see **3**), includes an apt quotation from the book of Psalms to highlight the overlap between these Christian and classical vocabularies: *In manibus portabunt te ne forte offendas ad lapidem pedem tuus* (In their hands they shall bear thee: lest perhaps thou knock thy foot against a stone) (Psalm 90:12).

A close examination of this section of the map demonstrates that some changes were made during the engraving process. The outline of a field boundary and some vegetation are visible as faint lines underneath the later composition. In this instance, the engraver was less than successful in burnishing out these lines and marks to make space for the new artwork. Revisions were also made to other parts of the map. This is especially evident in the area of Prospect Hill where the outlines of previously-engraved houses and a tree are visible as faint lines.

Fig. 6: The faint outlines of earlier engraved work are visible in this section of the map, present Prospect Hill.

4. A LANGUAGE OF DEFERENCE – THE CLASSICAL DIMENSION

GALVIENSIS
DESCRIPTIONIS
Declaratio.

Galway in the early seventeenth century was a vibrant and prosperous metropolis. Although small in comparison with other Irish port towns, it was – in the words of one contemporary writer – 'built in the manner of a tower' and possessed 'fair and stately buildings. The fronts of the houses (towards the streets) are all of hewed stone up to the top, garnished with fair battlements in a uniform course, as if the whole town had been built upon one model. The merchants are rich, and great adventurers at sea . . . and in their manner of entertainment and in fashioning and apparelling themselves and their wives they preserve most the ancient manner and state'. This approving description finds its full-length portrait in the pictorial map, which is a celebration and promotion of the historic town in all its extraordinary detail.

The map imparts a sense of grandeur to its streetscapes which, densely packed with houses, are intended as tangible expressions of the self-confidence and aspirations of a thriving and secure community. Urban tower-houses such as those belonging to the Lynches (S) and Athys (R) point to the time of their emerging administrative and ecclesiastical independence in the later fifteenth century (see **16**, **17**, **18**). But these and other similar tower-like structures shown on the map would give way to more comfortable residences, better suited to the trading and mercantile lifestyle of their inhabitants. The public street façades of their houses were enlivened with windows and doorways richly carved with ornament while heraldic plaques bore testament to the owner's ancestral lineage. Over time, outbuildings around one or more courtyards to the rear were added to serve the accommodation needs of the merchant's household and to provide storage for merchandise; some were also rented out as tenements.

The wealthy inhabitants assimilated what fitted into their own aesthetic, which, to a large extent, was embedded in the architecture of the Elizabethan and Jacobean worlds. The resultant generalised symmetry of building design and materials has led some commentators to see this as reflecting an innate conservatism. The reality was more nuanced, however, and the extensive trading contacts brought not just new goods but new ideas and fashions. While much of the physical medieval urban fabric and streetscape remained intact, many buildings were repurposed or rebuilt to showcase the latest styles, something that would have resonated with foreign visitors. The surviving Darcy (a) and Browne (d) houses testify to the extensive renovation and remodelling of existing dwellings in the earlier seventeenth century (see **19**, **21**). Innovations in form and design are evidenced in the town house of Sir Robert Lynch (V; see **6**), on the corner of Shop Street and Abbeygate Street Lower. This is a building very much in the new mode of architecture with its exaggerated curvilinear gables and oriel window pointing to an acquaintance with the latest architectural fashion in vogue in northern Europe. And to further impress the viewer with their Renaissance flair, many houses are depicted with ornate rear gardens. At this period urban gardens were generally modest and of a functional nature, providing plants for medicinal, culinary and household use. Those depicted on the map, for the most part, are laid out in a formal Renaissance style. Their geometrically arranged plan with a central circular bed and ornamental trees is suggestive of a low-hedged parterre with intervening walks. It seems likely that the compilers employed this schematicism to highlight the sophistication and status of the wealthy house owners. These are places of intimacy and enclosure away from the hustle and bustle of the streets, invoking sentiments of a civilised world and a cultured people.

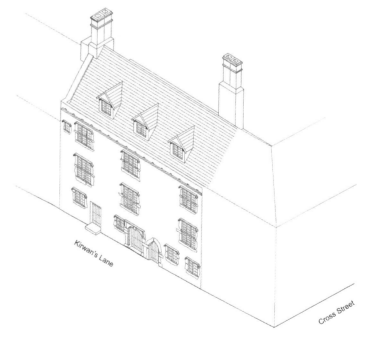

Fig. 7: Isometric reconstruction of a house in Kirwan's Lane (based on surviving fabric) showing a typical seventeenth-century frontage (Office of Public Works).

5. GALWAY'S 'FAIR AND STATELY BUILDINGS'

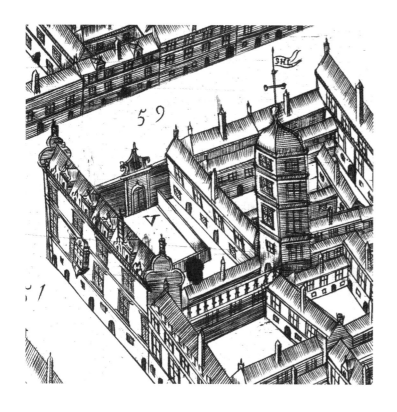

59

V

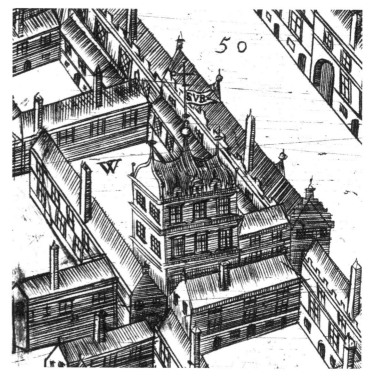

50

W

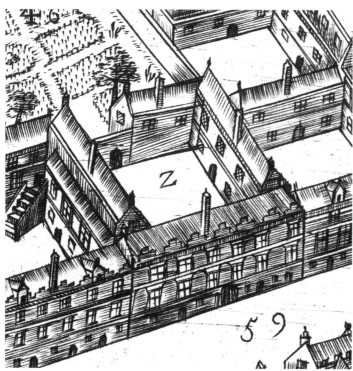

46

Z

59

&

D

R

By the early years of the seventeenth century Galway was ruled by a small group of wealthy merchant families whose members, through intermarriage and alliance, dominated the political, commercial and social life of the town. Ties of patronage, friendship and family bonds ensured that their confessional differences were masked in the interests of corporate control and mercantile advantage. The town houses of ten of these individuals are named on the map: Sir Robert Lynch, baronet (V); Sir Valentine Blake, baronet (W); Sir Peter French, knight (X); Sir Richard Blake, knight (Y) Sir Dominick Brown, knight (Z); Sir Oliver French, knight (&); Mr. Martin Darcy, citizen (a); Sir Walter Blake, knight (b); Mr Anthony Ro Lynch, citizen (c); and Mr Martin Brown, citizen (d).

There are limited biographical details available for nine of these townsmen but the documents of the period are lacking in contemporary references to the tenth, Mr Anthony Ro Lynch, though his inclusion suggests that he was well-connected. The surviving evidence suggests that all of the named individuals were Catholic even if their loyalty to Rome did not always accord with the views espoused by its papal legate, Rinuccini, in the late 1640s. Some indication of the intricate network of the dynastic alliances that permeated the Galway patriciate in the middle of the seventeenth century is attested by the marital and family relationships of four individuals (names in bold signify those identified on the map; see also **20**).

Top left, V: The town house and buildings of **Sir Robert Lynch**, baronet (on the corner of Shop Street and Abbeygate Street Lower). Sir Robert Lynch (d. 1667), lawyer and politician, was the eldest son of Sir Henry Lynch (d. 1635) who with **Sir Richard Blake**, both lawyers, administered the business interests of Richard, 4th earl of Clanricard. Robert was mayor of Galway in 1638–9. He married a daughter of **Sir Peter French** and was brother-in-law to **Sir Valentine Blake** (3rd baronet) and to Patrick Darcy and Richard Martin, two of Galway's most prominent lawyers. He was father-in-law of Dominick, the second son of Andrew Brown, brother of **Martin Brown** (see **19**).

Top right, W: The town house and buildings of **Sir Valentine Blake**, baronet (on the north side of William Street). This property undoubtedly belonged to Sir Valentine, 3rd baronet (d. 1652), MP for Galway borough in 1640 and mayor of Galway in 1643–4. His father, Thomas Blake, 2nd baronet (d. 1642), was married to a sister of **Sir Dominick Brown**. Valentine married a daughter of Sir Henry Lynch (d. 1635) and was brother-in-law to **Sir Robert Lynch**.

Bottom left, Z: The town house and buildings of **Sir Dominick Brown**, knight (on the east side of Abbeygate Street Lower) stood across the street from those of his first cousin, **Martin Brown** (see **19**). Dominick Brown (d. c. 1656) was MP for Athenry in 1634 and mayor of Galway 1634–5. He married a daughter of James Riabhach Darcy (d. 1603), was brother-in-law of **Sir Peter French** and **Martin Darcy** (see **21**) and father-in-law of **Sir Oliver French.** His brother, Fr Valentine Browne OFM, was guardian at the Franciscan friary, Galway (see **28**), and provincial of the order in Ireland. His eldest son, Geoffrey, was a noted lawyer and member of the supreme council of the Catholic confederation.

Bottom right, &: The town house and buildings of **Sir Oliver French** (on the north side of Market Street). These buildings are partly obscured by Athy's Castle (see **18**). Sir Oliver French (d. c. 1666), mayor of Galway in 1650–1, and **Sir Valentine Blake** were two of the four hostages detained by the Cromwellians at the signing of the articles of surrender in 1652. Oliver married (as his second wife) a widowed daughter of **Sir Dominick Brown** and her sister married Sir Oliver's eldest son, by his first wife.

Fig. 8: Entry for the year 1643 (Galway Corporation records, Liber A, fo. 182r) highlighting the name 'Valentyn Blake junior' whose house is referenced on the map (*W*) (JHL).

6. THE GALWAY PATRICIATE

38

32

4

14

F

F

15

23

ANGELIS
MANDAV

Su
Mun
1 Antemur
Propugnac
2 Septentrion
3 Medii muni
4 Australe cornu
5 Antemuralia circa
5a Munimeſu in quo
6 Munimeſu antiquar
7 Munimeſu ſiue aggec
8 Vetus propugnaculum
9 Locus ſupra Mola Ma
Tia caſtra ſupra treſpo

74

25

One of the most striking aspects of this map is the fact that, with the exception of the two ecclesiastics standing in the courtyard of the College House (see **23**), the core urban space lacks any human or animal presence. A small number of figures have been included on the town's peripheral elements such as the two sentries on the gun emplacement at the New Tower (see **9**), another on top of Ceann an Bhalla and two individuals at the tiled exchange beside it (see **10**). Even the quays are deserted despite the large number of ships berthed there: not a single person is to be seen. While the absence of humanity from streetscapes is not unusual for maps of this period, in this instance there is little doubt that this was an intentional artistic device that was used to focus the viewer's attention on the map's central component – the town in all its municipal and ecclesiastical splendour.

This picture of a depopulated town is in marked contrast to the representation of the world outside the walls where the countryside is enlivened with vignettes of ordinary men and women going about their everyday lives. The underlying symbolism is clear: these are pointers to a bountiful hinterland, one that not only supplies the town with all the necessities of life but supports a thriving export economy. Goods and produce are brought to market by boat, wagon, barrow or basket; cattle, sheep and horses are husbanded in the fields, grain is harvested and the bay teems with an abundance of fish (see **38**). The vision of pastoralism in harmony with nature is alluded to in the depiction of the herdsman who, accompanied by his dog, is shown taking a break from his daily chores. Sitting on a rock with his staff by his side he is shown playing a tune on the shawm, an oboe-like woodwind instrument that was very popular in Renaissance times. Activities such as hunting (see **37**) and fishing (see **11, 36**) are depicted in detail and, while the wealthier citizens play ball-games (see **30**) or tilt at the ring on the Green (see **29**), young boys amuse themselves with swimming in one of the town's mill races. The elements have been carefully selected to instil in the viewer a feeling of communal well-being, a sense that all is right with the world. This is a place where peace and prosperity reign and where the social hierarchies are protected and sustained by a sovereign monarch.

Fig. 9: A horse-drawn covered wagon makes its way downhill towards town (top); a barrow-load of timber(?) is brought to market (middle); a woman carrying a basket of produce on her head (bottom).

7. A BOUNTIFUL HINTERLAND

One of the weakest points of any fortification is the entrance area or gateway. In consequence, these were usually provided with additional protective mechanisms, which, at the larger castles and towns, took the form of an outer forework or barbican. Such a structure was built at Galway in the 1270s together with the Great Gate as part of the initial walling of the town. It is depicted on all early plans and is specifically identified as a 'barbican' on the earliest map of the town by Barnaby Googe in 1583.

It is described in the map index as 'The old rampart before the Great Gate, commonly known as *Obair an Sparra* [i.e., the work at the town gate]' and depicted (*6*) as having a parapet and narrow wall walk. The latter, however, must have been wide enough to accommodate artillery for when Sir William Russell, the lord deputy, came to Galway in November 1595 'four great pieces of ordnance were discharged on the outer wall, without the gate of the town'. Directly below the wall walk were a series of arched embrasures pierced by arrow-loops. The central rounded perforations suggest that they were subsequently modified to accommodate firearms after these came into common use in Ireland in the sixteenth century. This forework possessed two opposing entrances set in the sides (*29*) and only when one came through these could access be gained to the Great Gate (*30*), which was further protected by substantial timber gates and an iron portcullis.

Some additional work was undertaken on the gate (*17*) in 1638 when the sources record that 'the east tower gate of the hour clock was built upon the cost of the corporation'. This appears to refer to the erection of the clock structure whose face is visible in its

Fig. 10: Detail from the plan of Galway, *c*. 1691, by J.N. Bellin (rotated) showing the new entrance through the fortifications to the north (bottom) of the forework (NLI).

west gable. The bell on top was rung to let the inhabitants know when the gates were opening or closing. It was used also at times of celebration or danger, as in 1642 when it was rung to warn the townspeople, who were then besieging St Augustine's Fort (see **24**), that a sally was being made by the fort's garrison. The swallowtail flag flying from the cross above the bellcote displays the initialism SPQG, signifying 'The Senate and People of Galway', a word play on its original Latin form *Senatus Populusque Romanus*, that is also found in the map's dedicatory inscription (see p. 5).

During 1650–1 the forework was fronted by a substantial bastion (*3*), part of the large-scale defences erected by the inhabitants on this side of town (see **9**). A small portion of this bastion survives and can be seen in Ballalley Lane. Both the forework and its surrounding bastion – depicted as two separate entities on the map – were amalgamated into a single structure by 1685, by which date the Great Gate appears to have all but disappeared. These works were probably undertaken in 1652 when two new bastioned citadels were erected by the victorious Cromwellians. The Upper Citadel was constructed so as to block off access to the Great Gate, thereby ensuring that all traffic had to pass through it. Over time this proved bothersome for both the military and the inhabitants who, in 1686, requested that an opening be made through the fortifications. Accordingly, a passage was broken through the eastern ramparts immediately north of the Great Gate, named 'St James' Gate' in the contemporary corporation records. This resulted in a kink in the main street at this end, one that survives to the present day and that is reflected in the name of the victor in the ensuing war, Williamsgate Street.

8. THE GREAT GATE, FOREWORK AND BASTION

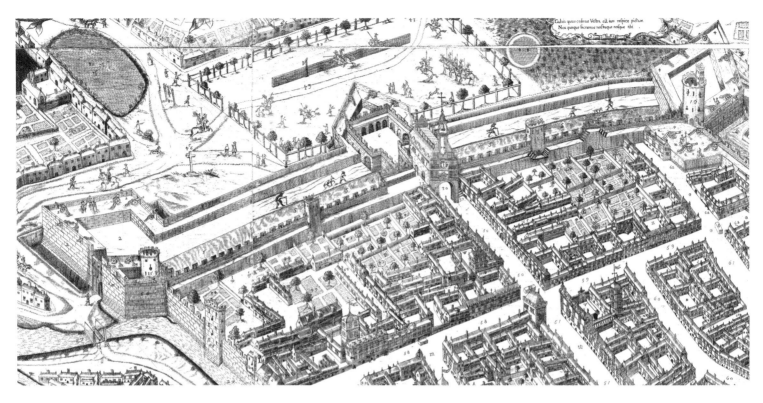

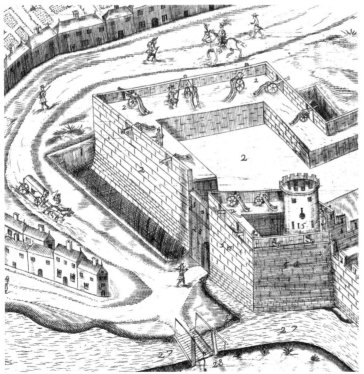

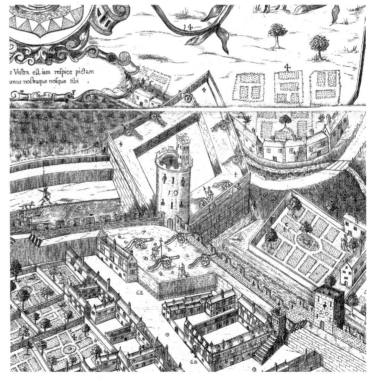

One of the defining characteristics of a town in the medieval and early modern periods was its mural fortifications. In that regard, Galway's walls – though depicted on this map at a larger scale than the town's buildings to give them visual prominence – were not suited to the requirements of mid-seventeenth-century warfare. The decision by the townspeople to support the insurgents after the outbreak of hostilities in 1641 was to have a dramatic and lasting impact on the fabric of the urban landscape. Aware of the town's vulnerability on its east side they decided that this was best protected by erecting two large bastions at the northern and southern corners of the curtain wall. The Lion Tower bastion (*5a*), built in 1646, was intended to protect the northern suburb and adjoining town wall as well as providing flanking fire along the eastern curtain to the Great Gate (see **8**). The New Tower bastion (*4*), built in the following year, would provide corresponding flanking fire along the eastern and the southern curtains as well as offering protection to ships riding in the harbour. Any approaching army could expect to receive considerable offensive firepower from the artillery placed in these bastions and the map shows that the New Tower bastion was further strengthened by a substantial gun emplacement directly inside the town wall (*7*). Civic pride and confidence in these works are reflected in the surviving two stone plaques bearing the coat of arms of the town, which were inserted into each bastion.

But this confidence was shaken when Cromwell introduced large siege artillery into the war in 1649. The recognition of its effectiveness in the reduction of Drogheda and Wexford undoubtedly was a factor in influencing the Galway inhabitants to make further improvements to their defences. Military engineers were clearly of the opinion that the recently erected bastions were insufficient to protect the east curtain from a sustained and heavy artillery bombardment. In consequence, the defences on this side of town were

supplemented by further bastioned outworks (*2*, *3*). Their construction, extending over 70 m east of the town wall, would have necessitated the clearing of a substantial area of ground on this side and, as is evident from the map, intruded on part of the Green that two decades previously had been railed in and planted with trees (see **29**). These works, erected in 1650–1, were never tested but their formidable defensive frontage was sufficient to require the advancing parliamentary army to decide on a siege rather than attempt to take the town by battery and storm.

Fig. 11: The plaque from the Lion Tower Bastion bears the following inscription: 'This woork was made by the towne and corporacion in the year of Edmond Kirwan Fizt Patrick his mearalty 1646'.

Fig. 12: A surviving section of the Lion Tower Bastion, Eglinton Street, 1950s. The inscribed plaque (area digitally enhanced) is visible above the centre of the lean-to shed. The remains were demolished in 1964–5 (NMS).

9. BASTIONED DEFENCES

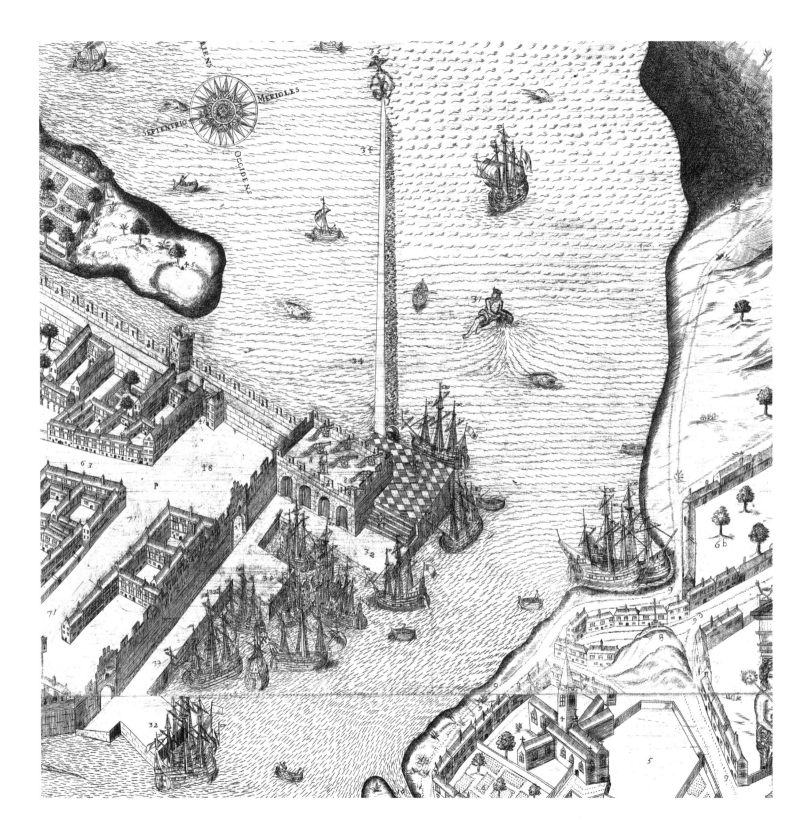

The prosperity of medieval towns was determined largely by their strategic location, good communications and access to trade routes. Galway possessed these geographical advantages to the full and had become – as noted by the Irish courtier, Sir Richard Bellings – 'the port where all the commodities in the province of Connaught that were transported beyond the seas were shipped and there the produce of them either in foreign wares or money was returned'. Central to this economic success were the quays (*32*), which were protected by 'the old bulwark near the strand, commonly known as Ceann an Bhalla' (*8*), present-day Spanish Arch. Though much modified over the centuries, including being converted for artillery use in the later sixteenth century, the core fabric of this structure with its four arched cellars probably dates to the time of the first walling of the town in the later thirteenth century.

The picture on the map of a busy port helps forge the impression that this was a hub of modern commerce. To reinforce this view, the quays and town walls are depicted as built with finely coursed masonry, thereby emphasising the strength and impregnability of the town and its infrastructure. The reality, however, was more mundane as attested by the plan and prospect drawn by Thomas Phillips in 1685 that show only one projecting quay element – not two as depicted on the map. The original strand stretched from outside the Old Quay Gate (*36*) at the south-western end of Quay Street to Ceann an Bhalla (*8*) and served as the berthing station for the shallow-draught ships of an earlier era that would enter at high tide and beach for unloading. Its existence is confirmed in the name recorded for Quay Lane on the map, Bóthar idir dhá Stranda – the lane between the two strands (*71*). A second entrance, the New Strand Gate (*37*), was broken through the town wall in 1537 and it is tempting to speculate that this was done to provide access to a recently added quay element. The northern quay, though depicted on this map, was not built until the close of the seventeenth century.

Attempts in the earlier seventeenth century to reclaim part of the saltmarsh to the east of the pier-like stone embankment (*34*) that projected southwards from Ceann an Bhalla to the Crow's Rock (*35*) came to nothing (for a depiction of this area in 1685 see **30**). By 1688 the corporation had converted this embankment into a pier and it was probably at this time that the archway was broken through to allow access to the new work. The erection of a new dock at the end of the Long Walk in the earlier eighteenth century, together with the building of a watch house for custom officials on the site of the two easternmost arched cellars of Ceann an Bhalla, points to a rising spirit of enterprise on the part of a number of local merchants.

The early years of the nineteenth century saw a fish-market erected on the northern quay and the area beside it filled in. Following

Fig. 13: Detail from Thomas Phillips's prospect of Galway in 1685 showing a less busy port and reflecting a decline in trade in the later seventeenth century (NLI).

the opening of the new commercial dock in 1842 (see **30**) the older facilities were no longer required and were removed as part of the mid-nineteenth-century drainage and navigation scheme. The remnants of these former quays now lie submerged beneath a covering of paved landscaping and grass. Only the carcass of the former storage cellars, decorously labelled the 'Spanish Arch', serves to anchor the viewer's perspective and provides a reference point to the city's seven centuries of maritime trade.

10. THE QUAYS

The 'great and only bridge, leading from the west into the city' – as described in the map index – the West Bridge (*26*), was erected in 1442 and replaced a pre-existing structure of much older date. Defended by three gates (*31, 32, 33*) that included a drawbridge and portcullis, it must have presented a formidable prospect to anyone approaching from the Iar Connacht side of the river.

This bridge is one of the most intriguing edifices depicted on the map and its representation must caution the viewer against the uncritical acceptance of everything depicted there. The walls of the gates and parapets present an almost cardboard cut-out appearance and are shown as equal in thickness. In addition – and contrary to the evidence from earlier and later plans and views – the gates are shown as open-ended structures rather than towers. Phillips's prospect, drawn in 1685, provides a more realistic impression of the remains, even if the central tower that housed the drawbridge (*32*) was then in ruins. It also shows the bridge as having a span of ten arches: only seven are shown on the map (the two mill-race arches are not included in either count).

Of particular interest are the tower and mill depicted at the west end of the bridge, one of the rare examples where the documentary record, artistic image and architectural remains are in mutual support. In 1558, a Thomas Martin was granted 'the site of a water-mill to be built on the lower part of the bridge of Galway; provided that within two years he should build, for its defence and security, a gate of suitable height and dimensions, and a tower of stone and lime, subject to the supervision of the mayor and bailiffs of the town'. A fortuitously surviving plaque with a contracted Latin inscription confirms that he had completed this work by 1562. This tower is represented on the pictorial map as a very tall narrow structure built up against the south side of the bridge but only the western corner of the attached mill building is visible.

The drawbridge had been removed by the middle of the eighteenth century and the arch built up, although both its tower and that at the end of the bridge still survived. The bridge survived for another century but was replaced by a new one in 1851 (renamed William O'Brien Bridge in 1889), built as part of the extensive drainage and navigation scheme undertaken at that time.

Putting to one side the issues of verisimilitude one cannot but be captivated by the image of the two men casting their tridents at salmon from the parapets of the Great Bridge, a practice that continued into the late eighteenth century. Providing an intimate insight into everyday lives, this practice was not without its dangers. In 1763 a man spearing salmon at the bridge was drowned when the cord got entangled about his legs.

Fig. 14: West Bridge from Thomas Phillips's prospect of Galway, 1685 (NLI).

Fig. 15: Stone plaque, with inscription: *Thomas Martin et Evelina Linche hoc opus mulindinumque fieri fecerunt A.D. 1562* – Thomas Martin and Eveline Lynch caused this work and mill to be made, A.D. 1562.

II. THE WEST BRIDGE

At the heart of every medieval town was the market place. The compilers of the Galway map were keen to highlight this aspect of the urban landscape, across several sites. Within the walled town 'seven public places or principal markets of the city' are recorded in the index. These specialised in the sale of commodities that included corn, fresh- and salt-water fish, meat, cattle and horses. Present-day Cross Street (Upper and Lower) is documented as the setting for the sale of various goods and wares. In addition to their primary function as locations for commercial transactions and exchange, they served as places for cultural encounters between the largely English-speaking inhabitants or their servants and the native Irish-speaking 'grey merchants' and market goers from outside the walls.

The principal market place (s; printed on the map as the 'long s', an early form of the lowercase 's' that resembles an 'f' without the cross-piece) was located at the major intersection, named Market Street (52), where the main thoroughfare, present-day Shop Street, opened into a wide fork to accommodate the streets leading to the quays and the West Bridge (see 10, 11). Described in the map index as 'The corn market where all other wares are sold without distinction', this open space was a symbolic embodiment of the urban hierarchies which, in 1514, determined that the mayor, warden and bailiffs were to be 'first served with all provisions' and after that it was 'who first comes is first served'.

The market place served as a place not only of exchange but also of administrative and social control. At its centre stood the market cross (Z), an emblematic expression of the duties and rights of buyer and seller and the place where public notices were proclaimed. To the west, the old tholsel (t; see 14) housed not only the rooms of the common council, but the fresh meat market or shambles. The proximity of St Nicholas's Church (see 22) undoubtedly reflects an early association between congregating in town for religious worship and the opportunities this gave to traders, most especially on church festivals. This municipal space was also the setting for the town's hospital or poor house for men (y), founded in 1504 and dedicated to St Nicholas. And when a site was chosen for a new tholsel in 1639 this central location provided the ideal situation (u; see 15). Also contained within this public space was the pillory – though not recorded on this map – one of the instruments of social control operated by the local magistrates. The cleanliness of the market place and, indeed, of all the town's streets depicted on the map, belies a reality that required the corporate officials in the later sixteenth century to prohibit the feeding of hogs 'within the town especially upon the market place'.

While the map highlights the more important localities for commercial exchange, it is distinctly lacking in details on core trades and services at the lower end of the urban hierarchy. Some degree of specialisation and clustering of individual crafts can be inferred from street names (e.g., Skinner's or Glovers' Street, Shoemakers' Lane, Fishermen's Lane). To these may be added the general artificers, bakers, boatmen, brewers, butchers, candle-makers, car-men, common labourers, cooks, craftsmen, distillers, fishermen, glovers, goldsmiths, harpers, horse-men, inn keepers, messengers, millers, porters, seamen, sellers, shoemakers, shop-keepers, skinners, tavern keepers, waggoneers and weavers, each of whose activities were recorded as needing reformation in 1585. Under the direction of their respective trade guilds, their lives revolved around the market, which acted as a levelling force within the community. It was their centre of congregation, of regulation and supervision and remained the principal means by which the daily life of all inhabitants continued to be sustained.

12. THE MARKET PLACE

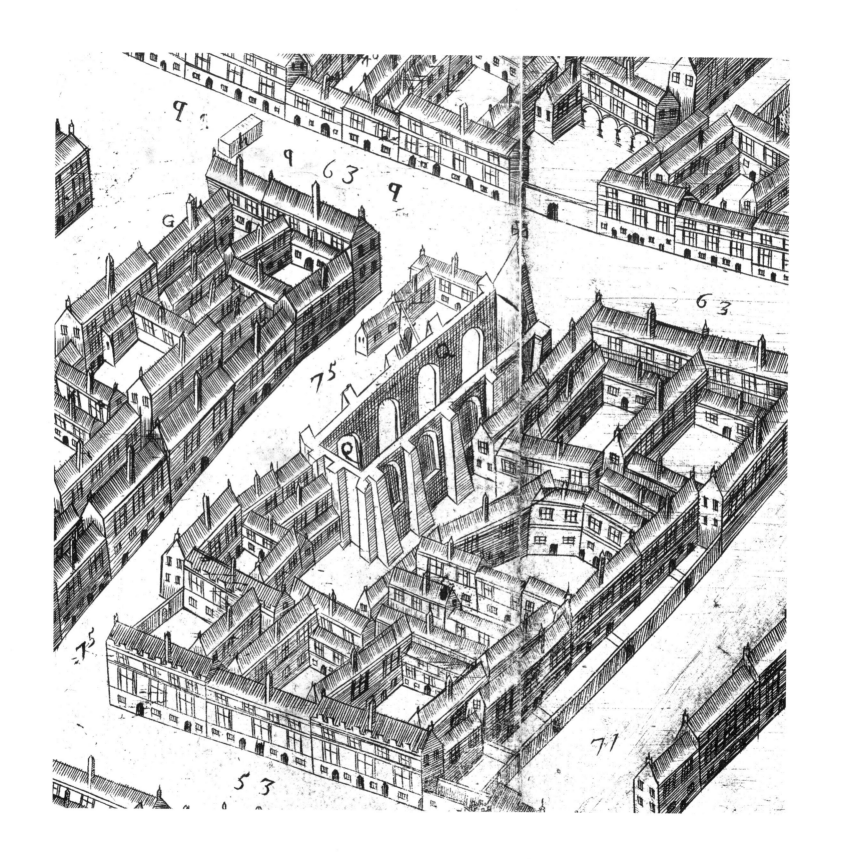

Described in the map index as 'The old buildings of the illustrious Lord, Richard de Burgh, the Red Earl' (*Q*), this ruin takes its name from Richard Óg de Burgh (d. 1326), one of the most powerful Anglo-Norman magnates in Ireland in the late thirteenth and early fourteenth centuries. His father, Walter, had died in 1271 in the castle at Galway, which was located to the west of the hall, and it appears that the latter edifice was built after the former had fallen into disuse. As the town began to be enclosed with walls in the later thirteenth century, the need to maintain a dedicated fortified residence became unnecessary and the requirements of a military administrative centre under private jurisdiction were no longer essential to the needs of an emerging borough. The large window openings represented on the map – clearly a stylised rendering of gaping holes in the masonry – indicate that the defensive considerations normally found in castles of the period had given place to a more refined architecture whose primary function was as a space for public government. Here the affairs of the town were regularised, taxes and rents gathered, disputes resolved and public justice exercised in the weekly courts.

Archaeological excavations undertaken on the site between 1997 and 1999 uncovered the lower courses of its east and west walls and confirmed its buttressed representation on the map. They also demonstrated that the building was refurbished in the fourteenth or fifteenth century and these works included a second phase of buttressing and the insertion of three centrally placed octagonal stone columns, replacing earlier timber ones. The date of the abandonment of the hall is unknown but it probably coincides with the decline of de Burgh power in Galway in the fifteenth century. The building, described in 1556 as a ruin, was reused as a centre for smelting and ironworking in the sixteenth century, as is testified by the archaeological finds and the imprint of a large cruciform anvil base uncovered during the excavations.

The historian Roderic O'Flaherty, writing in 1684, noted that its ruins 'called Clogh an hiarla [Cloch an Iarla] or the Earl's stone' were still extant. Its impact on the urban landscape at this period is reflected in the names of the adjoining streets recorded on the map: 'Earl Street or Sráid Tobar an Iarla' (*63*) and the 'Red Earl's Lane,

Fig. 16: Reconstruction of the hall, *c.* 1400 (J. Harrison & Associates).

commonly known as Bóthar an Iarla' (*75*). The cobbled surface of a further 'street' was uncovered during the archaeological excavations along its west side. This is not shown on the map and must have been built over by this time. For reasons that remain unknown, the artist has chosen to place a cross on its southern intact gable (at the junction of the two map sheets) perhaps pointing to a time when there was a less rigid separation of secular and ecclesiastical powers.

Following the rediscovery of the Red Earl's Hall in 1997 the new offices destined for the site were completely redesigned to allow for its preservation and the remains are invigilated as an educational and tourist attraction by Dúchas na Gaillimhe – Galway Civic Trust.

13. THE RED EARL'S HALL

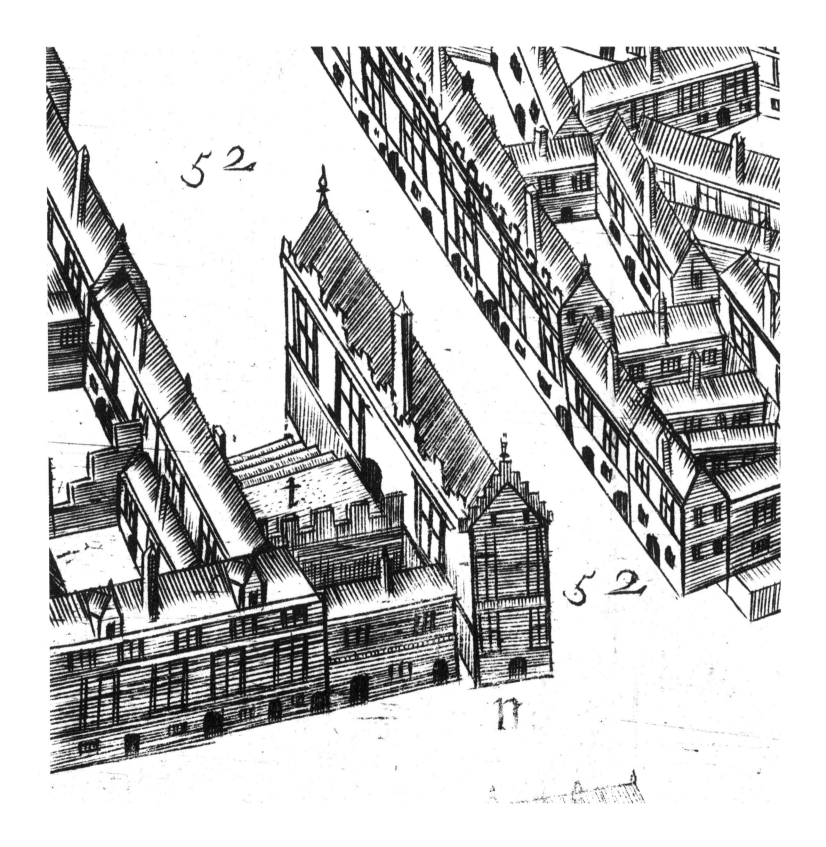

52

52

ŋ

The most significant improvement to Galway's municipal government occurred in 1484 when, under the charter granted by Richard III, the townspeople were licensed to elect annually a mayor, two bailiffs and a corporation. These new privileges bestowed a significant measure of self-government. The resultant enhancement in status and trade enabled the merchant families to erect lavish dwellings such as Lynch's Castle (see **17**), make additions to St Nicholas's Church (see **22**), found a poor house in the town and establish foundations for the Dominican and Augustinian friars (see **24**, **33**). It was not until the middle of the sixteenth century, however, that the citizens decided to erect a town hall (*t*), or to give it its contemporary name as recorded in the corporation records, a tholsel. Although work began on its eastern section in 1557–8, it was not completed until 1580–1. A certain mercantile pragmatism is reflected in the design of the completed edifice, for this building served a number of functions. The upper floor, approached via a broad flight of steps on its north side (*t*), housed offices and a large hall or chamber that was used by the corporation, the courts of law and for civic assemblies. The ground floor was divided into two separate areas: one was used

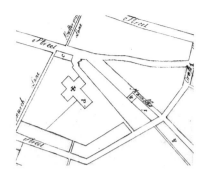

Fig. 17: Detail from plan of the town and fortifications of Galway, 1747 (rotated) showing the locations of the old and new tholsels (see **15**) and St Nicholas's Church (see **22**). Letters in the accompanying key identified as: c – Town house & Exchange; d – St Nicholas's Church; h – Old Barracks; i – City Gaol; k – Main Guard. Mainguard Street is named 'Shambles' on the map (BL).

for the town gaol and the other for the 'shambles', where animals were slaughtered and butchered for sale (*n*).

In 1639 the corporation decided to erect a new tholsel but the exigencies of those times prevented its completion (see **15**). When it finally was opened in 1709, the old tholsel was not only retained as a gaol and shambles but was used also as a main guard for soldiers, a function that is reflected in the surviving street name, Mainguard Street. At some point during the eighteenth century part the upper floor was used to house prisoners and the inspector general of prisons' report in 1796 recorded that this gaol was 'execrably bad, and what contributes much to its filthy and unwholesome appearance is a meat shambles kept underneath the prison'. Although the corporation passed various motions over the following years to have it demolished, this was not carried into effect until the new town gaol was completed on Nun's Island and the prisoners transferred there in December 1810.

The imprint of the old Tholsel can still be seen about mid-way along the north side of Mainguard Street where the buildings project forward of their neighbours to the east.

14. THE OLD THOLSEL

The increasing prosperity of the Galway merchants and landowners in the early decades of the seventeenth century found expression in the desire for a new town hall and, in 1639, the corporation decided to erect a 'strong, sufficient stone house, covered with stone slate, and to be underpropped with good stone pillars . . . the upper parts to be made a fair common hall or tholsel with convenient chambers for the Common Council and Town Clerk, for the safe keeping of all town records and writings'. This modern building, envisioned as a tangible expression of the enhanced municipal status granted by James I in 1610, was intended to be a focal point and it was fitting that the site selected be at the heart of the town – the market place. A number of stalls and shops beside the graveyard of St Nicholas's Church were demolished and work on the new tholsel (*u*) commenced in that year. It was continued and, as recorded in the corporation records, 'raised to a good height'

Fig. 18: Pen-and-wash drawing of the tholsel, early nineteenth century (GCCA, GS01/2).

in 1645 but construction then ceased, due no doubt to the urgent necessity to resource the improvements to the town defences (see **9**). When the Protestant interest took control of the corporation in 1654 it had neither the resources nor, it would appear, the desire to complete the building and it was to remain a ruined shell – as depicted on the map – for over fifty years.

Work resumed in the early years of Queen Anne's reign and various mayors contributed all or part of their salary towards its completion. The building was finished finally, in time for the inauguration there of the newly elected mayor on 29 September 1709. A good impression of the building can be gained from a watercolour drawing made *c.* 1800 that represents it as a simple two-storey structure with an open arcaded space on the ground floor. Fitted with seats along the back wall, this space was used by the townspeople as a place for walking and conversation and by the local merchants as the exchange. The upper floor accommodated a room for the grand jury and a large hall for meetings of the corporation and civic assemblies. The hall was fitted out as a court-room for the assizes and had a small gallery and jury room. The edifice was crowned with a hexagonal copula, its sides formed of large windows. The interior was fitted with seats and a dining table which, according to the historian of the town, James Hardiman (1820), 'was the scene of many a festive meeting' of the corporation. By the time he was writing, the tholsel had become dilapidated and, according to one commentator, the corporation transacted their affairs there 'at the risk of their lives'. The building was pulled down in 1822 much to the displeasure of some inhabitants.

15. THE NEW THOLSEL

Blake's Castle was situated in the south-western part of the town close to the strand and in the fifteenth century, the likely date of its construction, it would have had commanding views over the quays and harbour. As an example of a tall fortified house – a number of which are shown on the map – it is an urban relative of the contemporary rural tower house of the late Middle Ages.

Its position on the map coincides with the junction of four sheets and, in consequence, its representation has suffered. A comparison of the two surviving copies highlights inconsistencies in the management of the print process. On the TCD example – used in this extract – the corner of the copper plate for the eastern (left-hand) section of the castle did not fully come into contact with the paper and, as a result, the engraved lines are a little faint. The western part of the building on the adjoining sheet received a better impression. By a curious coincidence, the opposite is the case with the copy in the James Hardiman Library, where the corner of the right-hand plate appears not to have been adequately inked up. In addition, a hair or fibre (visible as s-shaped white line) appears to have fallen on the plate or paper during the printing of the TCD map. This does not occur on the Galway copy.

As with the two other named castles on the map (see **17**, **18**), the earlier history of this building is unknown. Described as belonging to William Blake in 1637, the property was forfeited in the mid-seventeenth century and granted to the Morgan family, Cromwellian settlers from Wales. By 1686 it had been leased for use as the county gaol, which was moved from Loughrea to Galway around this time, and it continued to function as such for the next 125 years. In 1788 it housed fourteen criminals in 'two long rooms with dirt floors and no fireplace' and four debtors were lodged in smaller rooms on the upper floors. The gaol was closed in 1811 and the prisoners transferred to the new county gaol on Nun's Island. In the nineteenth century the building served as a corn store and a substation for an electrical transformer in the mid-twentieth century. The surviving southern façade was 'restored' to a semblance of its former glory in the 1990s when it was converted to commercial use.

Fig. 19: View of Blake's Castle with a section of the town wall in the foreground, late eighteenth century (NLI).

The representation on the map would lead the viewer to interpret it as having a 'square' ground plan, typical of such tower-house castles. But this is incorrect and is undoubtedly due to the fact that its representation is split between two map sheets. Its battlemented upper section is visible on Phillips's prospect of 1685 (see **10**) and a further drawing of it survives from the closing years of the eighteenth century. Archaeological investigations on the site in 1990 revealed it to be a very substantial building measuring a little over 7.8 m along the street frontage and 14 m in depth. Its owners evidently were very conscious of the need to protect themselves and their merchandise for it was heavily defended at roof level with bartizans or small projecting towers at each corner and a machicolation in the centre of the façade directly above the entrance.

16. BLAKE'S CASTLE

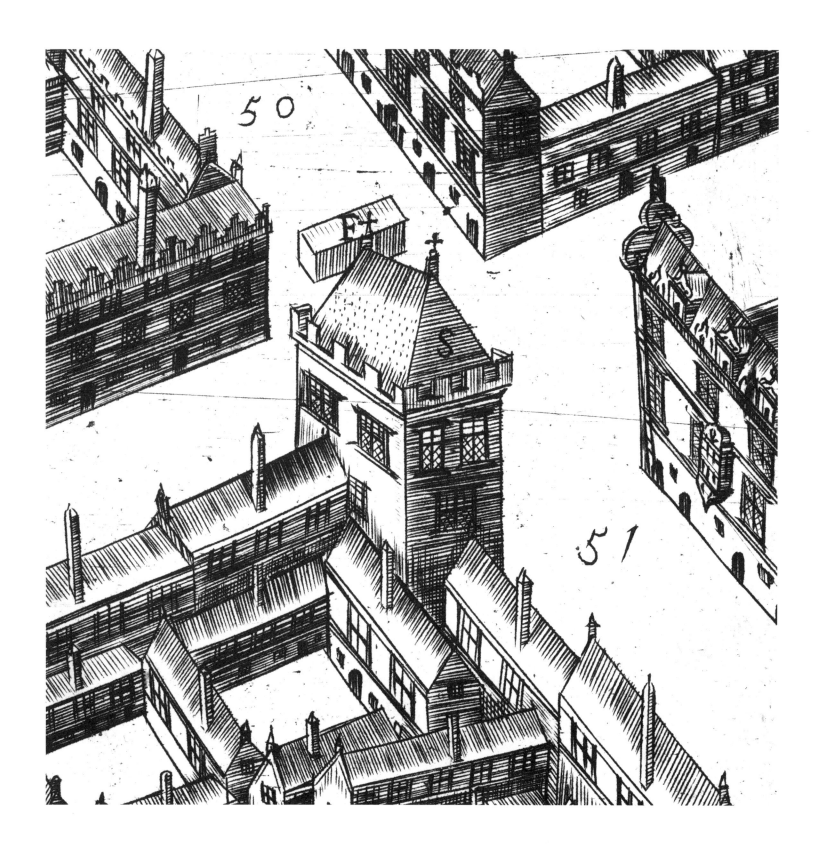

Situated at the junction of Shop Street and Abbeygate Street Upper – at the principal cross-roads of the old medieval town – Lynch's Castle (*S*) provides a glimpse of the architectural elegance that was typical of many Galway houses in the late Middle Ages. It speaks of a time when mercantile success enabled the wealthy Galway elite to erect lavish dwellings that not only offered security and comfort but served as mechanisms for the display of their social status. Even in the mid-seventeenth century this building must have presented an impressive sight to visitors, as it still does today.

Dating to *c.* 1500 and standing five storeys in height, this tower house epitomises the successful transformation of a defensive archetype to the requirements of urban domesticity. In contrast with many of its rural contemporaries – where decoration was mostly confined to interior features – the street façades of Lynch's Castle display an impressive array of carvings and heraldic panels, practically all of which have been repositioned in the course of the various alterations to the fabric over the centuries. In consequence, it is impossible to know whether the large Tudor-style windows depicted on the map in its upper storey are the product of the artist's imagination or represent the original configuration.

Nothing is known about the early history of the castle and it is not recorded by or for whom it was erected. The arms of the Lynch family, together with those of King Henry VII (1485–1509), adorn the Shop Street frontage while those of the FitzGeralds of Kildare are set near the corner of the Abbeygate Street Upper façade. The latter undoubtedly alludes to the assistance given to the townspeople by Gerald FitzGerald, the lord deputy, when he defeated the forces of Ulick Burke at the battle of Knockdoe in 1504. The gratitude of the townspeople is also attested in the two biblical inscriptions which, while expressing orthodox Christian ideologics, visually reinforce their appreciation to the deputy: *Post tenebras spero lucem* – After darkness, I hope for light (Job 17:12) and *Deposuit potentes de sede et exaltavit humiles* – He hath deposed the mighty from their seat, and hath exalted the humble (Luke 1:52), a quotation that is also to be found on the doorway of Martin Darcy's house (see **21**).

The box-shaped structure (*F*) shown on the map as almost blocking the middle of Great Gate Street (*50*), present Shop Street, refers to one of seven temporary altars, which, as set out in the index, were 'solemnly erected by the clergy in the streets for the festivity and procession of Corpus Christi'. This feast was celebrated in the Catholic liturgy on the Thursday after Trinity Sunday (eight weeks after Easter) and their inclusion on the map undoubtedly reflects Fr Joyce's yearning (see p. 5) for that time in the 1640s and early 1650s, when the Catholic inhabitants publicly celebrated their faith without restriction or hindrance (see **26**).

Fig. 20: Lynch's Castle, *c.* 1875 (Chetham's Library, Manchester).

17. LYNCH'S CASTLE

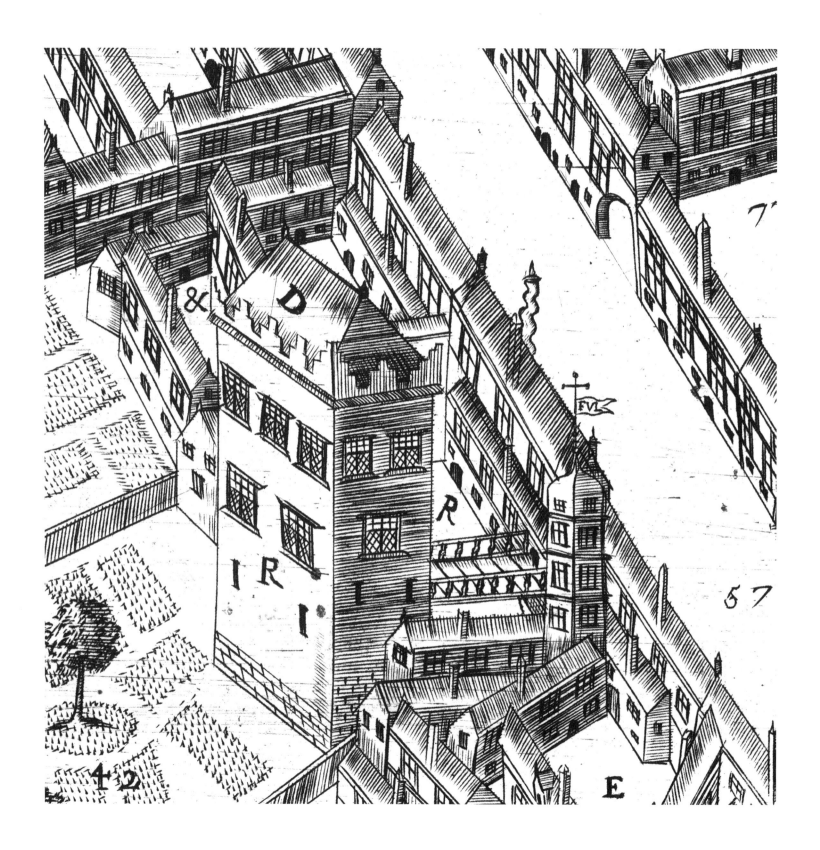

Fig. 21: Athy doorway, dated 1588, originally in St Augustine Street and now in Galway City Museum
(H.G. Leask, *JGAHS*, xviii (1938–9), p. 168).

Set back from the main thoroughfare of North Street (*57*), present-day Market Street, and rising to at least five storeys, Athy's Castle (*R*) must have been a very prominent landmark in this urban core. The narrow slit windows depicted in its lower storeys point to a time when considerations of defence were paramount, even for those living within a walled town. The fact that access appears to have been gained at an upper floor level via a wooden bridge from the buildings fronting the street further indicates the preoccupation with security. The hipped roof is framed by stepped battlements typical of Irish tower house construction and the castle probably dates to the fifteenth century or perhaps earlier. The upper floors are lit by large Tudor-style windows with contrasting square and diamond-shaped panes – also shown on Lynch's Castle (see **17**). These are noteworthy in highlighting the wealth of its owners, glass being an expensive commodity. They were undoubtedly later insertions in the upper floors and reflect the comfort of more settled and secure times. The significance of the capital letter 'D', that is prominently displayed on the roof, is unknown.

Nothing is known about the early history of the castle though its massive size suggests that the Athy family had achieved considerable commercial success and status. Only two members are recorded as holding the post of chief magistrate in the fifteenth century. A dispute between the Blake and the Athy families *c.* 1440 (resulting in the death of many members of the latter) has been interpreted as accounting for the fact that their power base and influence were never sufficient to enable an Athy to be elected to the office of mayor in the succeeding centuries. Nonetheless, the surviving ornate doorway, dated 1588 and bearing the Athy coat of arms and a merchant's mark, testifies to the wealth of at least one member of this family.

In the later seventeenth century the castle and adjoining property were in the possession of the Rutledge family who sold it to the crown in 1703. It acquired a new lease of life as the powder magazine for the Lombard Street barrack that was erected *c.* 1717. By 1760 its roof and floors needed to be propped as it was feared that the building would fall on the soldiers in the barrack beside it and, in 1769, it was recommended that it be demolished. This was carried into effect in the later part of that century.

18. ATHY'S CASTLE

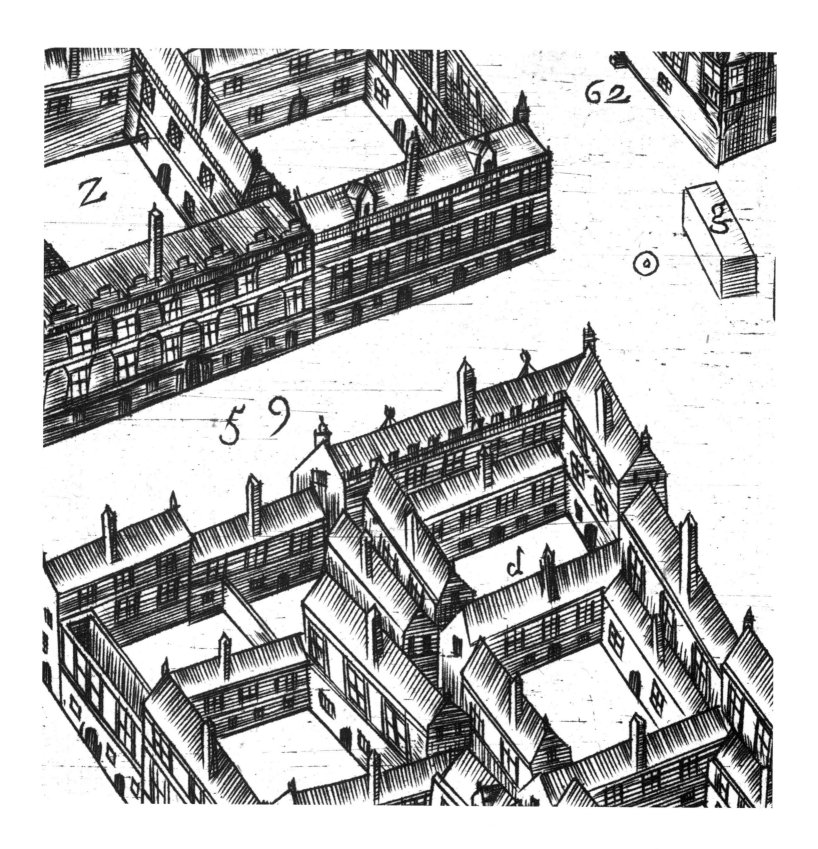

The town house of Martin Brown (*d*) was situated on the west side of Abbeygate Street Lower (Skinners' or Glovers' Street, *59*) at the junction with St Augustine Street (New Tower Street). Sir Dominick Brown, his first cousin, lived across the street (*Z*; see **6**). The few biographical details confirm that Martin Brown came from a resolutely Catholic family. His father, Oliver Brown fitz Dominick, was deprived of the office of mayor in 1610 for refusing to take the oath of supremacy and his elder brother, Andrew (d. 1640), was deposed for the same reason in 1632 after having been elected sheriff. Two of his nieces joined the Poor Clare order and, in turn, served as abbess of their community in Galway (see **35**). The date of his death is not recorded but it appears to have occurred in 1636. The Brown family lost much of their estate at the time of the Commonwealth confiscations although his son, Oliver (d. 1696), secured a grant of their lands in Athenry barony, Co. Galway, under the Acts of Settlement and Explanation.

Martin Brown clearly was successful in his mercantile endeavours as is evinced by the substantial dwelling and outbuildings depicted on the map and, though no longer living at the time of its publication, his family were held in such high regard as to have his name associated with it. By historical happenstance, the doorway from his house was rescued from destruction in 1877 and re-erected in 1905 as the principal entrance to the park at Eyre Square, which, at that time, was enclosed with railings. The panel directly above the door is dated 1627 and bears his name and that of his wife, Mary Lynch, accompanied by their coats of arms. Embracing the latest mode of architectural fashion – the classically inspired Italian Renaissance style – the Browns, along with other Galway families, tailored its elements to their own requirements. Mirroring a feature found on the Darcy doorway at the northern end of town (see **21**), which had been erected three years earlier, the keystone of the doorway is anchored in a quotation from the Old Testament: *Nisi Dominus aedificaverit domum, in vanum laboraverunt qui aedificant eam* (Unless our Lord build the house, they have laboured in vain that build it) (Psalm 126:1). And to maximise the visual impact, the Christogram, IHS (denoting the first three letters of the Greek name of Jesus), is prominently centred between the owners' names and the date on the panel above the door.

The doorway now stands in detached isolation at the northern end of Eyre Square since the railings were removed from the park in the 1960s. Protected by steel and perspex, it reminds the modern viewer of an older world and other values.

Fig. 22: Entrance to the town house of Mr Martin Brown, Abbeygate Street Lower, *c.* 1875.

19. THE TOWN HOUSE OF MR MARTIN BROWN, CITIZEN

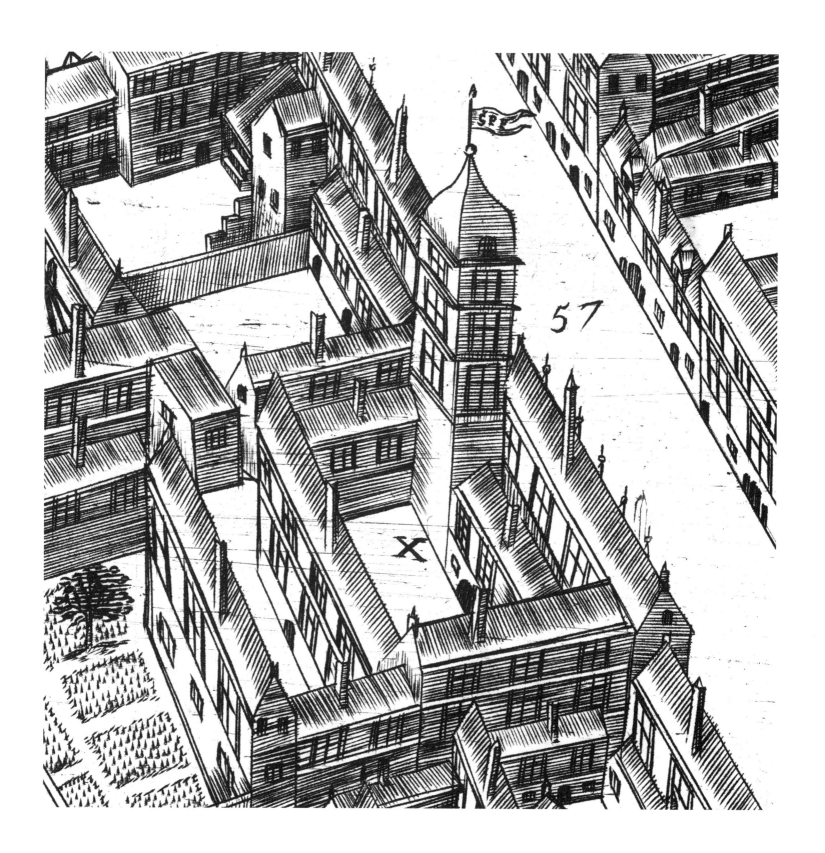

eter French fitz Valentine came from a family who had been prominent in Galway's municipal affairs for at least three generations. Both his father and his grandfather were mayors (in 1592 and 1565 respectively) and, in due course, Peter was elected to this office in 1616. Refusing to take the Oath of Supremacy, he was disbarred from holding that office for life and fined £100 for his recusancy. Despite his undoubted Catholic sympathies, he was knighted in August 1623 by the lord deputy, Viscount Falkland.

The intricate social networks that operated among Galway's mercantile elite are typified by his familial and marriage connections. His sister was married to Sir Thomas Blake (2nd baronet, father of Sir Valentine Blake; see **6**) and Peter married Mary Brown, the daughter of an alderman. Her brother, Sir Dominick Brown, also a leading merchant, lived in Lower Abbeygate Street (see **6**). The Frenches had three daughters, one of whom married the lawyer Patrick Darcy (the youngest brother of Martin Darcy; see **21**), and another married Sir Robert Lynch (see **6**).

As eldest son, Peter undoubtedly inherited the family town house on Market Street (*X*). This was a substantial property and typical of those belonging to other merchant families in having a courtyard around which were ranged further buildings and warehouses. In keeping with the prevailing fashion, they added a new front entrance to their house in the latest classical style, which was embellished with their coats of arms. As with a number of other prominent members of the Galway patriciate whose houses are referenced on the map, the flag flying from the top of the tower bears the device S.P.F., the initials of the words Sir Peter French.

From the later seventeenth until the early nineteenth century the house was leased by the Poor Clare sisters and, after they left in 1825, by a community of Augustinian nuns from 1839. The building subsequently went into ruin and was pulled down in the early years of the twentieth century.

Sir Peter French died on 27 February 1631 and was buried in the Franciscan friary (see **28**). His widow erected to his memory a large sculpted and painted monument at a cost of £500 sterling, which, according to a contemporary chronicler, was 'gilded with gold and all made of fine carved marble'. After the taking of the town by the parliamentary forces in 1652 this monument, along with many others, was broken up and part of it converted by the governor into a chimney. The two panels that survive in the graveyard of the Franciscan friary are tangible manifestations of Catholic piety in the earlier seventeenth century. As part of a much larger and ornate monument, they also served to testify in a permanent form the family's position in the local social hierarchy.

Fig. 23 (left): Entrance doorway to Sir Peter French's house, Market Street, photograph, *c.* 1875 (Chetham's Library, Manchester).

Fig. 24 (above): Panel with the impaled coat of arms of Sir Peter French (left, d. 1631) and Mary Browne (right, d. *c.* 1659) flanked by two figures in bishop's robes with their right hands raised in benediction. On the left St Patrick, with the double patriarchal cross, crushes two serpents as a grotesque devil figure flees from under his feet and, on the right, St Nicholas holding a crozier, is accompanied by one of his associated symbols, a child rising from a font; a theological reference to the legend in which the saint resurrected the dismembered remains of three boys from a pickling barrel.

20. THE TOWN HOUSE OF SIR PETER FRENCH, KNIGHT

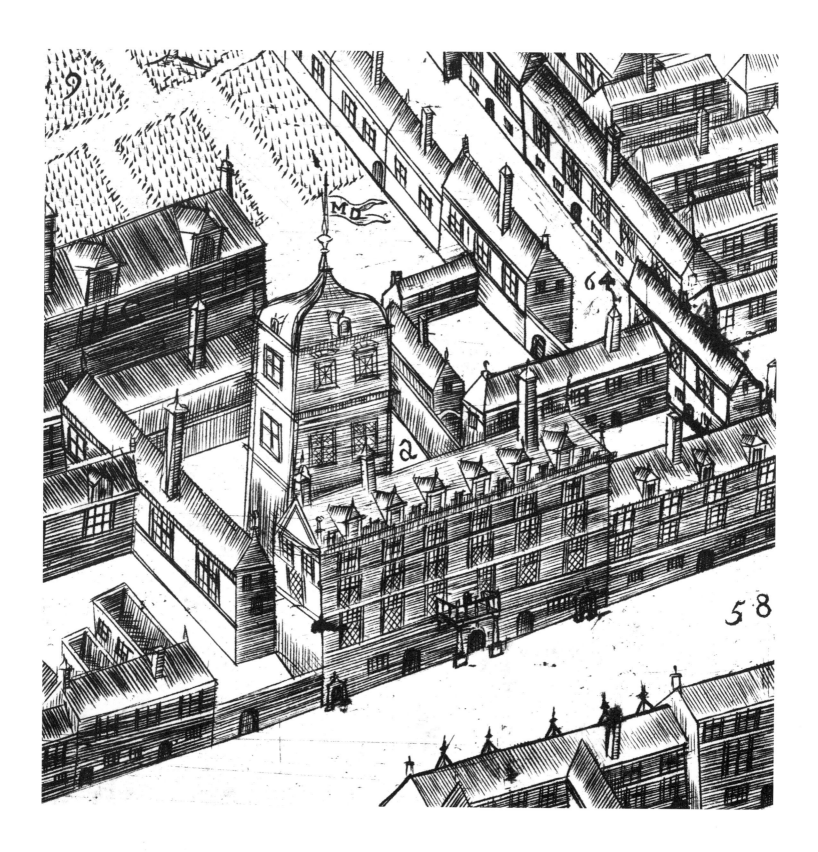

Martin Darcy was the second of seven sons of James Riabhach Darcy (d. 1603) who was vice-president of Connacht in Elizabethan times. As the eldest son produced no issue, the extensive estates were settled on Martin who married Christick Martin, daughter of Alderman Richard Martin. Darcy fell foul of the lord deputy, Sir Thomas Wentworth, when, as sheriff of the county in 1635, he impanelled the jury that found against the deputy's proposed plantation scheme for the county. Having been imprisoned in Dublin, he died there in June 1636, reportedly as a result of ill-treatment.

The wealth of the Darcy family is reflected in the size and extent of their town house (*a*) that is represented as a six-bay, four-storey building with dormer windows in the roof space. In common with the many 'fair and stately buildings' in Galway (see **5**), various other out-offices and structures were ranged around a courtyard to the rear. Attached to the house is a tall tower – undoubtedly a former tower-house type structure – which is capped by an ogee-hipped roof: its finial flies a flag displaying the owner's initials, M.D. The adjoining property to the rear (*C*) was occupied by Mr Anthony Ro Lynch (see **6**). Although the Darcy house has disappeared entirely, its principal doorway was rescued and re-erected in the grounds of the Sisters of Mercy, Francis Street. While it may no longer retain its railed balcony – as depicted on the map – the surviving remains bear a certain versimilitude with the artist's representation.

Dated 1624, the doorway embodies the aesthetic aspirations of the wealthy Galway merchant families in the first half of the seventeenth century. Wishing to emulate the elegance of such grand houses as that owned by the earl of Clanricard at Portumna, Co. Galway, the civic elite embraced this 'new' classicist architecture in a way that afforded them further opportunities to display their ancient lineages. The coats of arms of both families, accompanied by their respective initials, are given equal prominence in the spandrels on either side of the doorway and the inscription spread across the scrolls directly below them (a place normally reserved for the motto) proudly proclaims *Quod Deus conj[uxit] homo non separet* (Which God hath joined together, let not man separate) (Mark

Fig. 25: Doorway, dated 1624, from the house of Martin Darcy and Christick Martin, in the grounds of the Sisters of Mercy Convent, Francis Street.

10:9). Whereas Martin Darcy and his wife might look to England and the Continent for expressions of social architecture, they clearly looked to Catholic Rome for their religious belief and observance, something they were not afraid to declare to the public at large. The keystone of this remarkable doorway, with its distinctive Bacchanalian mask, is positioned rather incongruously at the centre of a quotation from the *Magnificat*, the canticle of the Virgin Mary recorded in the gospel of St Luke (1:52): *Deposuit potentes de sede et exaltavit humiles* (He hath deposed the mighty from their seat, and hath exalted the humble), an inscription that, coincidentally, is also found on Lynch's Castle (see **17**). This devotion is emphasised by the Christogram (IHS) and Mary's name (MARYA) in the spandrels flanking the bottom of the keystone.

21. THE TOWN HOUSE OF MR MARTIN DARCY, CITIZEN

Dedicated to the patron saint of sailors and merchants, the parish church of St Nicholas was both a physical and a spiritual presence at the epicentre of the medieval town. The building speaks to the history of Galway through the centuries and, with its surrounding graveyard and tall broad-leaved tree, was placed centre stage on the map as a reminder to viewers that this was the focus of a shared world, serving communities in solemnity and celebration. The map index provides a detailed list of the fourteen altars that were located in different parts of the church, distinguished by the following letters in italics:

A. The choir in which stood the high altar dedicated to St Nicholas.
B. The chapel of the Blessed Virgin Mary (the south transept).
C. The chapel dedicated to the Most Holy Sacrament.
D. St Anne's Chapel (the north transept).
E. St Patrick's Chapel (to the north of the choir).

The church did not address the street directly and was accessed from 'An Céim Cam – the crooked path' (*77*) that ran behind houses on Market Street and Lombard Street and skirted its walled-in graveyard (*x*). The exceptional width of this 'street' is partly a cartographical invention that serves to showcase the church. This edifice provides one of the few holdfasts on the map that can be used to test its representational accuracy. Apart from the omission of the slender tower adjoining the west corner of the south transept, the structure bears a remarkable resemblance to the fabric that survives today, something that undoubtedly may be attributed to Fr Joyce's (see p. 16, note 37) intimate knowledge of the building (for a cautionary note on the map's accuracy in its depiction of other features, see **10**, **11** and **27**).

Although the church was at the very heart of the town and its community, since the middle of the sixteenth century it served only the Protestant members of the divided confessional congregations. By the early 1640s this division became even more pronounced when the tensions between parliament and king erupted into rebellion. In Galway the merging of Catholic and Royalist sympathies resulted in a dramatic and significant chain of events that led to St Nicholas's Church and the three friaries being repossessed for Catholic worship. For Fr Joyce and the other Catholic inhabitants, Sunday 18 June 1643 must have been a memorable day. This was the occasion when mass was celebrated for the first time in almost ninety years in their parish church. That there had been some rearrangement of the internal fittings during the previous period is indicated by the fact that a portable altar had to be erected there for the event. This was a celebration not just of a religious triumph but of a military victory over the pro-parliament garrison in St Augustine's Fort (see **24**). These successes were short-lived and after the surrender of the town in 1652 the church and college were returned to Protestant worship. They were again in the hands of the Catholic townspeople for a brief period during the Williamite wars (1689–91) but thereafter were restored to the Protestant community and the church is now a Church of Ireland (Anglican) parish church.

Fig. 26: St Nicholas's Church, *c.* 1814, by P.J. Haverty (NLI).

22. ST NICHOLAS'S CHURCH

Since its foundation in the thirteenth century St Nicholas's Church (see **22**) had been served by a priest appointed by the abbot of the Cistercian monastery of Knockmoy. Following numerous complaints about the quality of the incumbents, the church was established as a separate vicarage in the 1380s. In the next century there continued to be frequent disputes between the various applicants and appointees. This issue was finally resolved in 1484 when the archbishop of Tuam, Donatus Ó Muireadaigh (O'Murray) – who in 1446 was at the centre of a dispute about his own appointment as vicar – regularised the whole affair. He raised the church to the status of a college to be governed by a warden and eight choral vicars: this was confirmed by papal bull in 1485. The archbishop took the most unusual step of giving the responsibility for the appointment of the warden and priests (to be elected annually) to the local corporation. This was an exceptional arrangement for he effectively excluded – whether intentionally or not – his successors from the right of visitation. It became a matter of serious controversy over the following centuries and ultimately led to the dissolution of the wardenship (as it came to be called) in the nineteenth century.

John Lynch fitz Edmond, who was mayor of Galway in 1494–5, is recorded as building part of the college house (*B*) and a John Lynch fitz John bequeathed monies towards the work in 1496. Dominick Duff Lynch (d. 1508), who had been instrumental in securing the requisite papal approval from Rome in 1485, is also credited as one of its principal founders. The distinguished historian and native townsman, Fr John Lynch (d. 1677), recorded in 1669 that Dominick's coat of arms was to be seen above the college gate.

With the adoption of the Reformation in Galway the citizens secured a charter from Edward VI in 1551 establishing their church as the Royal College of Galway with authority to use a seal. Though the seal itself is lost, the surviving impression shows St Nicholas as bishop accompanied by three kneeling maidens, a reference to the legend that he had saved them from ruin by throwing three bags of money (shown on the seal to the right of the saint) in through their window. Not only did the warden and vicars exercise the cure of souls in the various parishes, but the duties of the clerk of the college also included having to teach the many poor boys who were accommodated there to sing at service in addition to allowing him teach other youths.

In 1643, the Catholic townspeople repossessed the church and college, which was then in a dilapidated state, and undertook various repairs. It became the residence for visiting ecclesiastical dignitaries and scholars. The papal nuncio, Giovanni Battista Rinuccini, resided there while in Galway in 1647 and again in 1648–9. The celebrated antiquary, Dubhaltach Mac Fhirbhisigh (d. 1671), records that he was staying there in 1647 when he undertook translations into Irish for the Poor Clare community at Galway (see **35**). It was here also that he compiled the main portion of his *Leabhar genealach* or 'Book of genealogies' in 1649–50.

Fig. 27: The seal of the collegiate church of St Nicholas.

By the early nineteenth century the college had been converted into several tenements and leased to various families. The building was eventually demolished in 1836, although a relic of its former collegial grandeur – the reader's desk that probably graced the refectory – was preserved and re-erected at the entrance to the Blessed Sacrament chapel in the church, where it remains to this day.

23. THE COLLEGE OF PRIESTS AND PASTORS

At the time this map was being printed, both St Augustine's Fort (*4*) and the Augustinian friary (*2*) were but a memory, the former having been demolished in 1643 and the latter in 1645. This may account for the fact that the alignment of the fort as depicted on the map needs to be corrected by about twenty degrees in an anti-clockwise direction so that the salient of the bottom right-hand bastion points to the middle end of the ridge.

The fort, first built in 1602, took its name from the friary, which was the last Augustinian foundation in Ireland before the Reformation. The Austin friars had come to Galway in 1508–9 and were to remain in occupation at their friary for the following fifty years. Given its prominent position on top of the ridge (named St Augustine's Hill (*4*) on the map) immediately south of the walled town, the friary's siting featured in almost every consideration of the town's defences in the later sixteenth century. It was here, in 1588, that some three hundred Spaniards, survivors of the ill-fated Armada, were killed.

Despite the defeat of the Spanish and Irish forces at Kinsale in 1601, the impending threat of a further invasion was the catalyst that led to the building of St Augustine's Fort in the following year. Constructed of earth and faced with stone, the fort soon began to slide and additional works were undertaken between 1608 and 1611 under the direction of Sir Josias Bodley, director-general of the fortifications and buildings in Ireland. These included the construction of a further stabilising outer tier and fosse, a gate-house, drawbridge and accommodation for the garrison and its commander, all of which

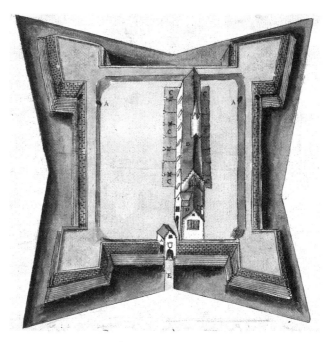

Fig. 28: Plan of St Augustine's Fort, 1608–11 (BL).

he documented on his plan. He also partitioned the church so that the chancel could be used for divine worship and the nave as a store.

Following the outbreak of hostilities in 1641, tensions between the fort's commander and the townspeople eventually erupted into open conflict. The fort was besieged in 1642 and again in the following year: it finally surrendered in July 1643 and shortly afterwards the fort was slighted. The church was spared and handed back to the friars, but considerations of defence necessitated its destruction some two years later. The fort survived as a large earthwork into the later seventeenth century (see extract from Thomas Phillips's 1685 prospect in **30**), at which time burial recommenced on the site. By way of containing the burial ground, the landowner walled in the upper section in 1811 and this was extended southwards to the roadside in the middle of the century.

Allowing for some realignment of the fort and buildings, the plan of St Augustine's Fort by Josias Bodley, 1608–11, is remarkably similar to that depicted on the map, though the northern extensions (drawn as a transept) to the church and captain's house are not shown on his plan and so must have been erected after this time. Bodley's plan is accompanied by the following key: 'The fort hath a double wall of stone wth a space of five foot between them into which ye sallies are at y^e letter A. B a church wch serveth for munition and store along the sides whereof y^e soldiers lodgings are built marked C. D: the Captain's lodging. E: a drawbridge' (BL).

24. ST AUGUSTINE'S FORT AND FRIARY

Among the many problems facing municipal authorities in the medieval and early modern periods was the management of infectious diseases. This was especially pertinent in port towns such as Galway, where incoming ships brought various maladies including the dreaded plague. Such was the concern at Galway that in 1521 a by-law was enacted ordering all ships coming to the town to be kept in quarantine for a number of days 'for fear and dread of the pestilence and common diseases'. The corporation also maintained a plague hospital outside the walls, which was situated near the junction of the present Dyke and Headford roads. Other than the brief reference to it on this map, very little is known about this establishment.

The social conscience of the civic authorities is attested by the provision of a hospice for citizens reduced to poverty due to age and infirmity. In 1542 the city fathers erected 'the Spittle or St Bridget's house in the east suburbs [4d5] . . . as maintenance to some of the poor members of the town falling to decay, and upon every Sunday every burgess of the town was obliged to send a maid to collect alms for the said house which was usually afterwards observed'. Additional support was provided in the form of bequests that included the perquisites of an eel weir on the river, named 'Correybridy' (Cora Bhríde – Bridget's weir) and a 'Friday salmon' out of the weir.

It is very likely that St Bridget's House (7) was utilised as a hospital in the following year, 1543, when Galway was ravaged by the 'English sweating sickness' (sudor Anglicus), a mysterious and highly contagious disease, which caused the death of numerous townspeople. The building subsequently appears to have been retained as a house for lepers – a 'leper' being identified with anyone who suffered from a contagious skin disorder. For fear of contagion, lepers were never allowed to come into the town, let alone dwell in it, and a corporation by-law of 1516 allowed only their 'clerk' or 'headmaster . . . with their bell' to collect alms.

In 1597 St Bridget's House along with much of the eastern suburb were burnt down by the marauding forces of Red Hugh

O'Donnell. A list of corporation property dated 1637 describes it as 'The Spittle House or Leaper House of St Bridgett, in the east franchises, with some plots of land thereunto belonging': these included one named 'Gornelourne', a corruption of *Gort na lobhar* – the field of the lepers. The hospital appears to have remained a ruin until the late 1640s when it was repaired by a native of the town, Francis Kirwan (d. 1661), bishop of Killala. His biographer, Fr John Lynch, records how 'St Bridget's house [7], generally known to have been at one time inhabited by lepers, but within our memory entirely ruined, he rebuilt, and the holy chapel dedicated to the same Bridget [6], where once the lepers used to come for the sake of hearing mass, he constructed, and brought the walls to a considerable height, but, prevented by the violent times, did not bring it to completion'. In light of this description it is doubtful whether its representation on the map (6) can be taken as accurate. The depiction of a substantial edifice surmounted by an enormous central tower undoubtedly reflects a desire on the part of the compilers to maximise the visual impact of this charitable establishment in an idealised, Catholic Galway. Nothing further is known about St Bridget's House, though there are incidental references in the later seventeenth century to the recovery of plots of land associated with it. Indeed, its precise location is unknown. As depicted on the map, it may be located on the south side and towards the top of present-day Prospect Hill.

Mystery surrounds the four subrectangular grass-covered blocks depicted in front of the chapel and the other haystack-like feature in the middle of the highway to the northeast: their function is unknown. Nearby is a wayside cross (19), which is identified in the index as Leacht Mór ní hEidhin (Ms Hynes's monument). While this surname has an ancient pedigree in the county, it is not recorded on the map among the fourteen 'tribal' and associated families or among the names of the other Irish aristocratic houses on its borders. This document remains the only known record of this woman and the monument erected by her or in her memory.

Fig. 29: Plague hospital and garden *(24)*.

During the troubled times of the 1640s many religious orders in Ireland fled westwards as the English parliament gradually extended its control over the country. Among those who came to seek shelter in Galway were the Carmelites (1641), the Poor Clares (1642), the Capuchins (1643), the Dominican nuns (1644) and the Augustinian nuns (1646). In addition to these, the map records the residences of the Carmelite sisters, nuns of the Third Order of St Francis, the Rich Clares and three other hospices for 'devout women'. The Franciscan, Dominican and Augustinian friars had been in residence in the town since the dissolution of their monasteries and had been joined there by the Jesuits in the earlier seventeenth century. By the late 1640s the town, which had become a rallying point for the pro-Royalist Catholics, had such a substantial population of clerics and religious that the papal nuncio, Rinuccini, was able to remark in 1647 that he was able to 'perform my functions and processions in Galway as I should have done' in his home town of Fermo, Italy.

Following the burning of the Capuchin house at Mullingar, Co. Westmeath, two of the brethren came to Galway in October 1643 seeking permission to establish a foundation there. They resided first at the college house (see **23**) and in the following year moved into rented accommodation beside the Great Gate (*H*, visible in **8**). The capuchin authors of the *Commentarius Rinuccinianus* record that the Galway citizens introduced them to the town as a thanksgiving for the capture of St Augustine's Fort (see **24**) and other Catholic successes during the war.

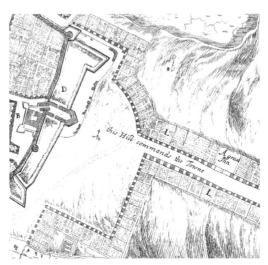

Fig. 30: The Great Inn
on Jones's map of Galway, 1691 (BL).

Fig. 31: The old dovecote in the south part of the town.

In 1650 they secured a site outside the walls on the north side of Prospect Hill (*8*). This residence is shown on the map as having a large courtyard – the only one depicted in the suburbs – with one side dominated by a church or chapel surmounted by a small bell-cote. These premises would appear to be the same as the Great Inn identified on Jones's plan of Galway in 1691. Both share the typical layout of coaching inns of this period, which were usually located on the outskirts of towns. After the surrender of Galway in 1652 the Capuchins, along with other religious, departed the town but they returned again for a brief period in 1689 only to be dispersed once more after its surrender in 1691.

Behind the Capuchin residence is a circular tower-like structure identified in the map index as an 'old dovecote' (*42*). There was a second similar structure inside the town walls to the south of present-day St Augustine Street and it is similarly described. The Latin adjective used for both is *antiquum*, which suggests that these structures were very old, dating to the early period of the town's history. Pigeons and doves have been reared as an important food source since Roman times and the custom of building dovecotes in Ireland was introduced by the Anglo-Normans. Such early examples as survive tend to be circular in plan with a slight external batter rising to a corbelled roof with a central opening through which the birds could fly in and out. Inside were rows of niches for the birds to roost. The two examples depicted on the map are akin to this form and have openings near the roof level – both have been dignified with crosses.

26. CAPUCHIN RESIDENCE AND DOVECOTES

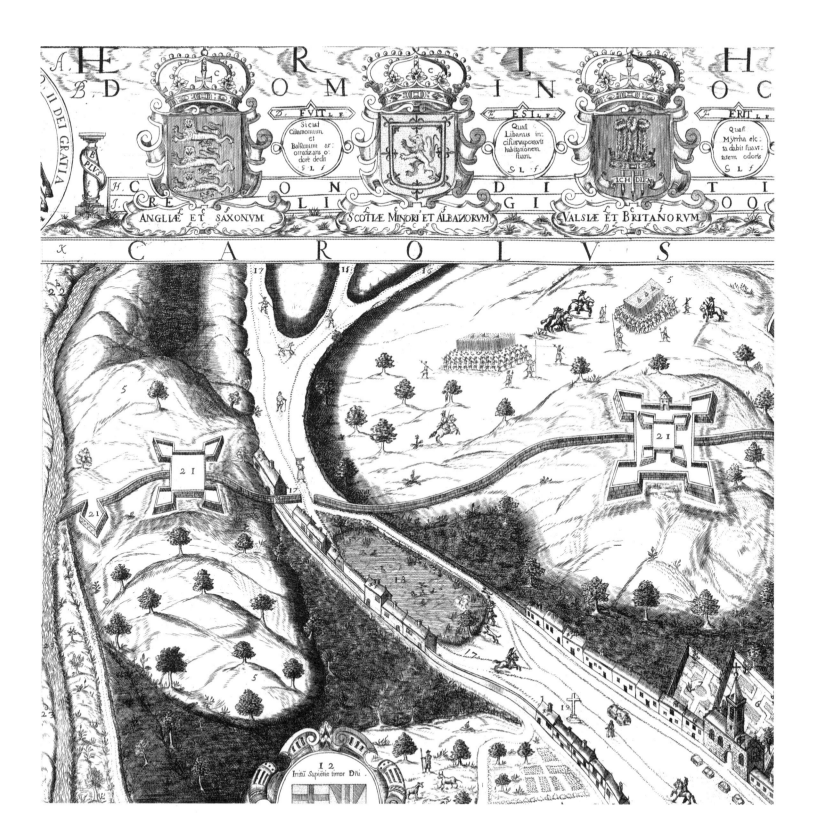

ÆHE R OM IN HO C

B D

II DEI GRATIA

B PLVS

D. FVIT L F

Sicut Cinamomum et Balsamum ar: omatizans o: dore dedi S L f

E ES L F

Quasi Libanus in: cisiusvaporavit habitationem suam S L f

F ERIT L F

Quasi Myrrha elc: ta dabit suavi: tatem odoris S L f

ICH DIEN

H C RE I ON LI GI DI TI OQ

ANGLIÆ ET SAXONVM

SCOTIÆ MINORI ET ALBANORVM

VALSIÆ ET BRITANORVM

X C A R O L V S

22

17 15 16

5

21

21

21

21

12

Initū Sapiétie timor Dñi

The mid-seventeenth-century wars in Ireland and England were marked for the most part, not by a series of open pitched battles, but rather by the taking of towns and cities by siege. When the campaigning season opened in Ireland, in spring 1651, the Royalist-Confederate forces were in severe difficulty as the parliamentary army controlled much of Ulster, Leinster and Munster. In May of that year Sir Charles Coote led his forces into Connacht and, having taken Athlone, brought his troops before Galway in early July. Recognising that the town was well defended with bastioned fortifications (see **9**) Coote decided on its blockade rather than attempt to take it by storm.

The parliamentary army constructed a line of entrenchments incorporating three detached forts (*21*) that stretched from the Suckeen bogs along the Terryland River (*23*) at the north-west to Lough Atalia at the south-east. These works were largely completed in early August when it was reported that Galway 'was shut up with 3 forts, [and] 13 redoubts'. The principal fort was in the centre, on the summit of the highest ridge which, together with that to the north, was then known as St Bridget's Hill (*5*). This fort commanded the main thoroughfare into Galway, An Bóthar Mór (Bohermore) (*17*). To the north-west and south-east were smaller forts linked to the central one by linear earthworks that, as suggested by the above account, were further fortified with a number of redoubts: a single example is depicted on the map close to the Terryland River (*23*). The blockade, supported by the parliamentary navy, who patrolled the bay, eventually succeeded and, after a nine-month siege, the town finally surrendered in April 1652.

The forts came to be used again during the Williamite war and, although repaired in 1690, did not form part of the defensive works at Galway. When the Williamite army came before the town on 19 July 1691 it is likely that they reoccupied these works as base-camps. But their sojourn there was short, for Galway surrendered two days later.

The siege works survived relatively intact until the later eighteenth century, as is attested by the 1785 survey of the Erasmus Smith estate by Thomas Sherrard. The lands around the northern fort had come into the possession of John Bollingbrook in the later seventeenth century and the fort became known under a corrupted form of his name, Boilingbrook Fort. Both the central and southern forts were removed by 1838–9 when the Ordnance Survey mapped Galway, but the northern fort and a section of the linear earthwork survived into the later nineteenth century: a small section is still to be seen off Seán Mulvoy Road.

The forts are stylistically represented on the map as faced with stone and each one has four diamond-shaped corner bastions. This, unquestionably, is a cartographical schematism used by the compilers to emphasise the strength of the besieging Parliamentary army. A more believable illustration of these entrenchments is to be found on Sherrard's plan of 1785, while excavations at the northern fort in 2000–1 established that stone facing was never part of its construction. In plan, its shape resembled a four-pointed star, typical of many such smaller earthen forts of the period. Unlike other contemporary representations of continental sieges, these works are depicted as devoid of both military personnel and artillery, though the besieging army is signified by mounted cavalry and two infantry detachments on the march in pike and shot formation (rows of musketeers surrounding the central core of pike men).

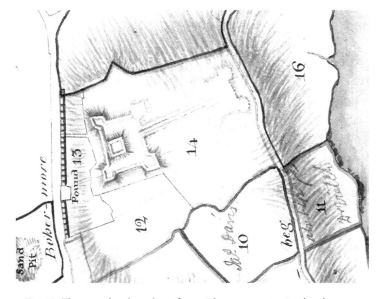

Fig. 32: The central and southern forts with a communication line between them. Detail from Thomas Sherrard's 1785 survey (rotated) (AES).

27. CROMWELLIAN SIEGE WORKS

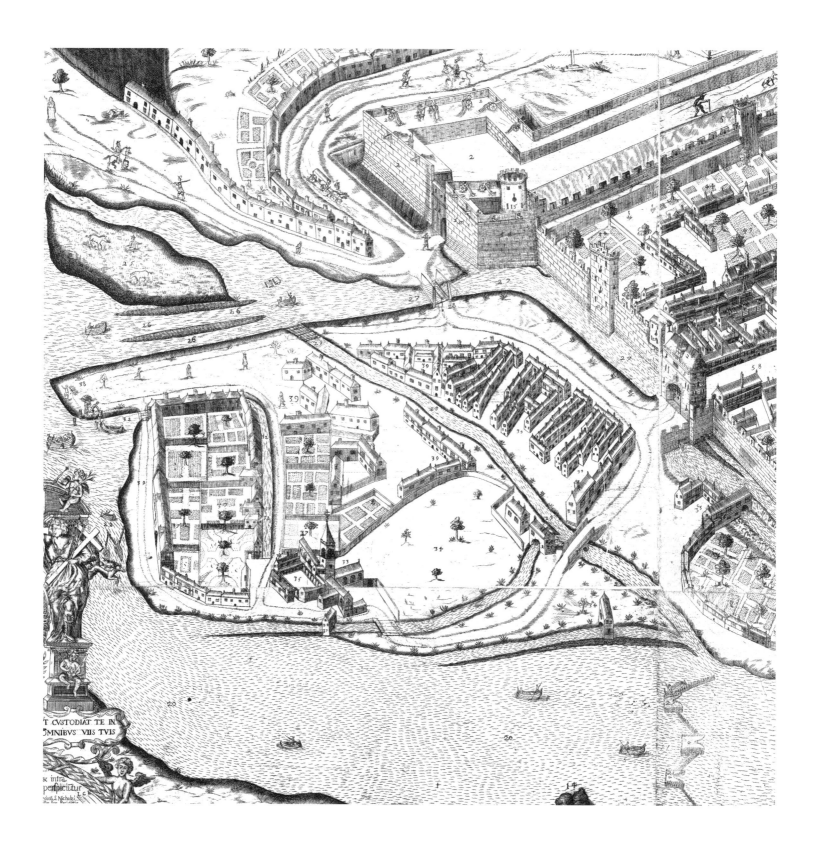

In the seventeenth century the northern suburb (*39*) encompassed three separate islands covering an area of about 13 acres (5.2 hectares) stretching west of present Woodquay and south to the rear of the properties on the south side of Mary Street and Bowling Green. The islands were bounded on the east by a watercourse that formerly ran through the centre of Woodquay to become the Little Gate River (*27*) that marked the northern boundary of the walled town. The embankments (*26*) depicted on the map reflect the ongoing efforts made to keep it open for navigation and the hand-operated drawbridge (*28*) indicates that boats probably came as far as the Little Gate (*34*). A proliferation of watercourses near the main river channel to the east powered at least four mills: St Francis' mill (*31*), Michael's mill (*3ᵃ4*), the Bridge mill (*3ᵇ5*) and the Little Gate mill (*3ᶜ5*).

At the north-east end of the suburb was Barr an Chalaidh (the top of the quay) (*38*), the upper end of the Woodquay. This quay played a pivotal role in the economic life of the town as boats brought produce and fuel from the shores of Lough Corrib to the Galway markets and returned with other necessary commodities. Following the opening of the Eglinton Canal in 1852 and the erection of a new landing quay to the north in 1858, the older quay went into decline and the river along its east side was gradually filled in and reclaimed.

The origins of the northern suburb are to be found in the establishment of the Franciscan friary (*33*) in 1296 on the island named after St Stephen. To access the 'Abbey' – a name still in use – from the town one had to cross three bridges; the first over the Little Gate River (*27*) that ran outside the town wall; the second, the Abbey Bridge (*30*), which spanned the river between the southern island and the narrow, triangular landmass to the north (known as Garryglass – An Garraí Glas); and the third, a wooden bridge that led directly to the west door of the church and the friary precincts. The Franciscan community were in possession of most, if not all, of St Stephen's Island which, in the earlier seventeenth century, contained extensive gardens (*37*) and houses for some forty people. An older watercourse (*32*), once used by the friars to ferry wood and other necessities to their monastery, had been reduced to a stream by this time. Their graveyard (*34*) became the chief burial place for many of the town's leading families (see **20**) and extended southwards from its present boundary, covering the area now occupied by Our Lady's College secondary school. Despite its dissolution in the mid-sixteenth century, the townspeople frequented the abbey to pray and bury their dead and continued to do so even after the building was repurposed as a county courthouse in 1610 under the charter granted by James I.

The map portrays a typical Franciscan friary of the period with the domestic buildings ranged around the cloister (*35*) to the north of the church. When the friars repossessed it in 1643 it is likely that they refurbished some of the buildings, although the work of reparation must have remained incomplete for both the north cloister walk and their refectory (*36*; Halla na mBráthar – the friars' hall) are depicted as roofless.

Confiscated under the Cromwellian regime the northern suburb, along with considerable other property to the east of the town, came under the control of the Erasmus Smith Trust (for the promotion of Protestant education), which, adapting to local circumstance, allowed the Franciscans to re-establish their community on its present site in the early eighteenth century. The legislative changes enacted in the later part of the century that enabled charities to grant longer leases provided the impetus to the board of trustees to develop their Galway properties. The gridded streetscape on Sherrard's map of this suburb in 1785 points to how subsequent growth in this new quarter, Newtownsmith, would progress over the following decades. The final integration of the northern suburb within the main urban space took place in the mid-nineteenth century when a section of the old town wall was demolished to make way for the new street, Eglinton Street, that linked with Francis Street.

28. FRANCISCAN FRIARY AND NORTHERN SUBURB

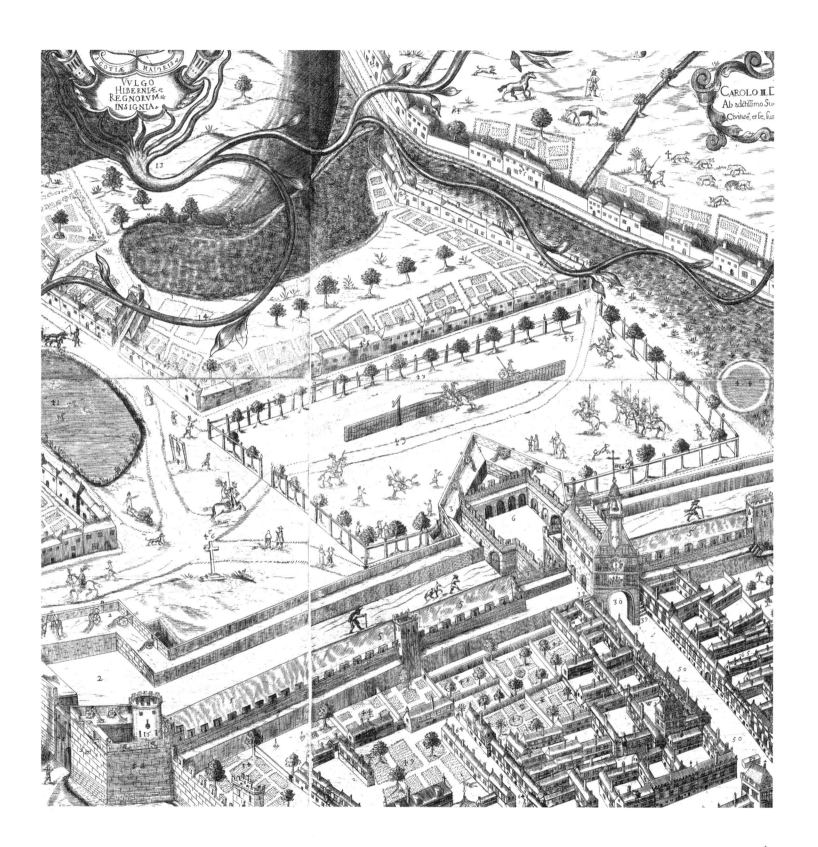

SCOTIÆ MAIORIS

VVLGO
HIBERNIÆ ⁊
REGNORVM
INSIGNIA

CAROLO II. D.
Ab adeliſſimo Stu
Civitate, et ſe, ſu

Eager to showcase their great civic amenity, the compilers of the map have enlivened this urban space with a wide range of activities and features. Originating as a large open area of common ground in front of the main gate of the medieval town, the Green (*43*) was kept free of buildings not only for reasons of defence but because it also served as a place for assembly and games. The festival of May Day was celebrated in Galway over three days and, on occasion, these revelries got out of hand as in 1620 when the fire from a musket resulted in a huge conflagration that started in the east suburb (*4ᵈ5*). The Green is referenced in the map index as the location in which 'the aristocracy of the city play on festive occasions' (*43*) and, to highlight their refined tastes, they are shown tilting at the ring, a form of jousting whereby a rider at full gallop attempts to insert a lance through a small metal ring or hoop. This was a popular sport in the seventeenth century among the nobility, especially in England and on the Continent.

This public space also was the location for a darker kind of spectacle. The representation of the town gallows with its single victim (*40*) indicates that such events were commonplace and the compilers had no compunction about including them in this portrait of the town. Nothing is known about the 'new market', referenced in the index as associated with the nearby cross (*4ᶜ6*), but the adjective would suggest that it reflects a relatively recent decision by the corporate authorities to provide an additional venue for trading purposes (see **12**).

An attempt by the city fathers at beautifying the Green's central area was undertaken in 1631 when it was enclosed with railings and planted with ash trees. There is little doubt that these were removed during the upgrading of the defences in the mid-seventeenth century (see **9**), as can be inferred from the significant intrusion of the middle bastion (*3*) into the park area. The inclusion of these embellishments on the map must be seen in the context of it being an 'historical delineation' (see p. 6).

Two further features depicted on the map are worthy of comment. The roughly level area at the northern end of the Green, at the bottom of present Prospect Hill, served as a catchment for rainwater and this muddy puddle became a significant topographical feature in its own right (*41*). The circular enclosure to the south (*44*) – unquestionably a cartographical schematism – is recorded in the map index as the 'place where, as it is said, the house of the Templars formerly stood': this map remains the only historical evidence for a possible Templar foundation at Galway.

This urban space continued to be known as The Green throughout the eighteenth century. It was later renamed Meyrick Square after General Thomas Meyrick, the military commander at Galway (*c.* 1800–2), who enclosed it with a stone wall as a parade ground for the local garrison. Members of the Eyre family had been in possession of this area since the later seventeenth century, and this no doubt contributed to it gradually becoming known as 'Eyre Square'. The name, however, was copper-fastened on foot of a lease of the property to the town commissioners by the then owner, Robert Hedges Eyre, in the late 1830s. The lease stipulated that the central area be enclosed with railings and developed as a classic Victorian park. The arrival of the railway and its associated hotel in the middle of the century ensured that Eyre Square became a hub of tourist and commercial traffic, while the open area at its northern end provided space for fairs and markets.

This recreational space underwent a further dramatic metamorphosis in the 1960s, when the railings were removed and the enclosed park was re-landscaped to accommodate car-parking. It was re-opened in 1965 and renamed John F. Kennedy Memorial Park in honour of the American president who had received the freedom of the city here a few months before his assassination in 1963. Further enhancements in the twenty-first century have attempted to encourage more urban concourse and revitalise the space as a focal point for the modern city.

29. THE GREEN

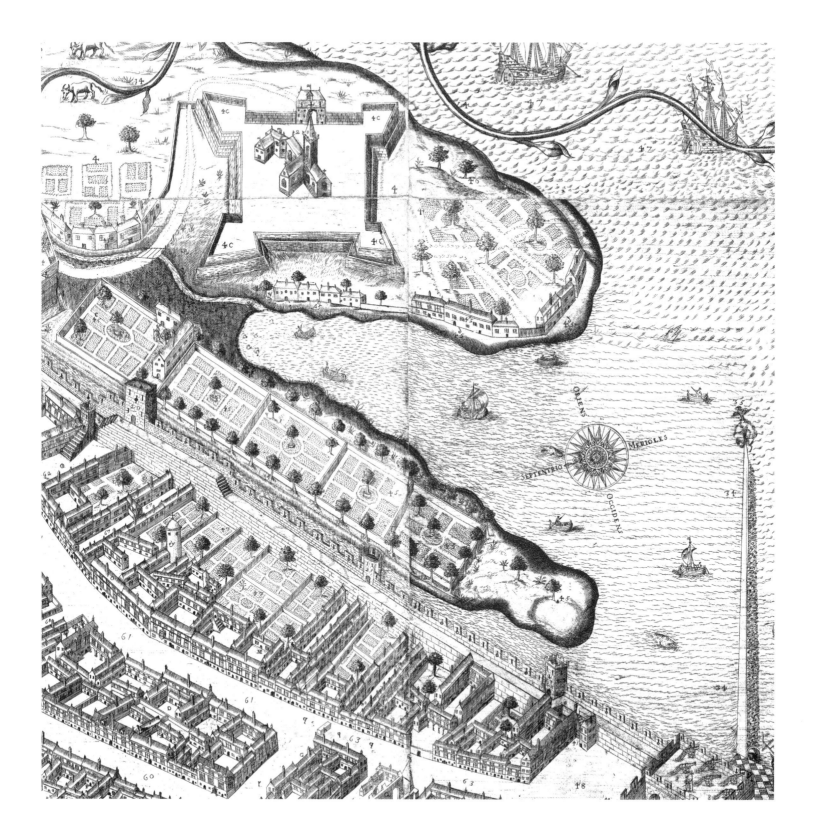

SEPTENTRIO · ORIENS · MERIDIES · OCCIDENS

Fig. 33: This detail from Thomas Phillips's prospect of Galway, 1685, provides a more realistic view of the gardens' angle (NLI).

The area to the south of the walled town comprised salt-marsh and mudflats that were covered by the tides and into which flowed the meagre outpourings of a small stream, the Meadle. Further to the south a number of dwellings, part of the eastern suburb (4ᵈ5), skirted the shoreline of the ridge on which stood the towering edifice of St Augustine's Fort (see **24**).

The tapering neck of land immediately outside the town wall is shown on the map as almost completely enclosed by four rectangular walled-in gardens framed on three sides by rows of trees (*45*). This area is described in the map index as 'The gardens' angle. Commonly known as Cluid na nGarrdha'. Though separated from the house and fifth garden to the east, the similarity in formal layout, with each containing a central ornamental tree in a tub-like container gives the impression that they all belonged to a single proprietor – perhaps the figure shown standing outside his house in the easternmost garden that has the added designation in the index as 'playing with balls' (*4ᶜ5*). As the man appears to be represented with a long-handled mallet over his shoulder this may reference the playing of pall-mall (ancestral to croquet), ground billiards or related games that were popular in the seventeenth century.

The depiction of these formal pleasure gardens, however, is in marked contrast to the view of this area drawn by Thomas Phillips in 1685. Even allowing for the neglect and deterioration that followed inevitably on the Cromwellian capture of the town, in 1652, it is reasonable to suggest that the representation of gardens on the pictorial map was exaggerated in order to showcase the recreational character of the town and the fashionable tastes of its governing elite.

By 1688 an attempt at improving the port facilities had resulted in the conversion of the narrow embankment of stone (*34*) into a pier, which, together with the new dock built at its southern end in the earlier eighteenth century, greatly improved the town's maritime infrastructure. The extensive area of saltmarsh and its adjoining properties had come into the possession of the Eyre family who began a process of reclamation that would eventually see the laying out of a new road, in 1779. This became known as Merchants Road on account of the numerous yards, stores and warehouses erected there. For many years there had been considerable discussion on the need for a new commercial dock to cater for the larger ships then coming to the port. Work on its construction began in 1833 and was completed nine years later, thus opening up the port for further expansion that continues to the present day.

30. FROM GARDENS' ANGLE TO COMMERICAL DOCK

The middle suburb (*13*) of the town, Ballymanagh – An Baile Meadhónach – corresponded with a small island of about 5.5 acres (2.25 hectares) whose topographical representation has been distorted on the map owing to the compilers' decision to give prominence to the extensive fortified works constructed there in the seventeenth century. In reality, the single thoroughfare depicted on the map, present Dominick Street Lower, roughly divides the island into two equal parts. This street acted as the principal artery of communication with Iar Connacht via the bridge at its southern end. The row of thatched cabins shown on Phillips's prospect of 1685 (see **32**) is a more convincing representation of the type of housing that must have been found here and in other suburbs.

At the time this map was being compiled the large bastioned fort (*48*) must have been little more than a degraded earthwork, as is suggested by its description in the index: 'The foundations of the western bulwark where formerly it was begun'. Work on its construction commenced in 1625 but it was never completed and the neat ashlar representation is unquestionably a cartographical convention. A similar method of construction is shown for the adjoining triangular fortification, a ravelin, which was erected outside the West Bridge in 1651. A more accurate representation of this area is provided by Phillips's plan of 1685, which shows the ravelin as a substantial earthwork with an outer dry fosse, though it is likely that a branch of the river was diverted into it for added protection when first erected.

This ravelin was refortified *c.* 1690 and again, by the Williamites, after the town's capitulation in July 1691. It had been entirely removed by the middle of the eighteenth century when a new thoroughfare was established along the eastern side of the island, enabling its incorporation into the larger process of suburbanisation that was gathering pace at this time. This thoroughfare would become known as Mill Street from the industries that developed in this part of the island. A new mill race was constructed across the northern part of the island and a paper manufactory was established there *c.* 1785 to be followed by the erection of extensive brewing concerns in 1816, named Madeira Island Brewery.

The improved economic and social conditions of the later eighteenth century are reflected in the number of new houses erected along Dominick Street Lower, praised in 1815 as 'uniform, spacious, elegant, and airy and forms a striking contrast to the gloomy grandeur of the clumsy and massive mansions' of the old town.

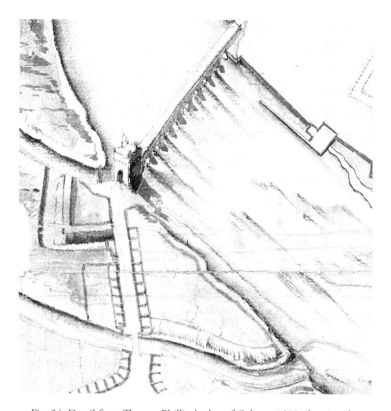

Fig. 34: Detail from Thomas Phillips's plan of Galway, 1685, showing the southern section of Ballymanagh (NLI).

31. THE MIDDLE SUBURB

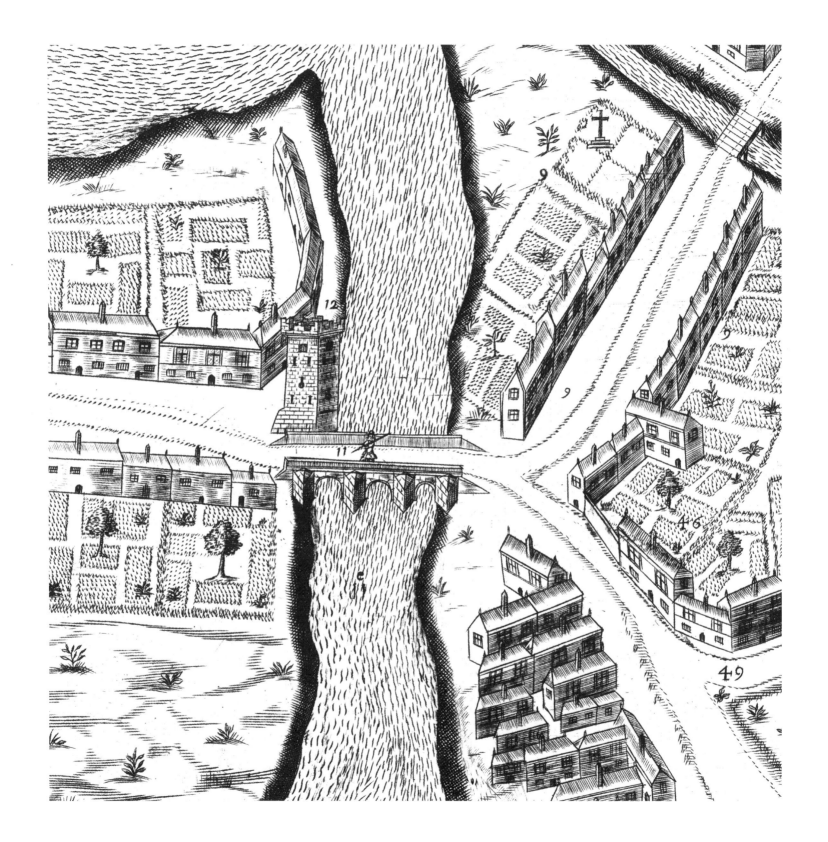

Prior to the establishment of Mill Street as a thoroughfare in the mid-eighteenth century the only means of communication by road with the southern suburb (*9*) and Iar Connacht was via this bridge. It was the focal point for all routes leading from the west (*49*) and north-west. Located at the south-western end of present Dominick Street Lower, this bridge gave access to Ballymanagh (Baile Meadhónach), the middle suburb of the town (see **31**). It is identified in the map index as the 'Bald Bridge, commonly known as Drochead Maol'. Although the Irish word *maol* could be interpreted as indicating that the bridge did not possess parapets, the map shows it with elegant examples; whether or not these were amplified in line with other cartographical embellishments cannot now be ascertained. It has been proposed also that 'maol' may signify that the bridge was not fortified, thereby distinguishing it from the principal West Bridge that was protected by three 'castles' or towers (see **11**). The presence of the fortified tower (*12*) standing immediately south of the bridge, however,

Fig. 35: Detail from Thomas Phillips's prospect of Galway, 1685, showing the southern end of the middle suburb with Balls Bridge on the left (NLI).

would suggest otherwise. Its name curiously shares the same descriptive adjective as the bridge: 'Jordan Castle, commonly known as Maol Chostain'. Its distinct castellated appearance and battered lower courses on the landward side bear comparison with many tower-houses and it may have served as some form of look-out tower. But this is merely conjecture for, other than its representation on this map, there is no other known reference to its existence.

Bald Bridge, corrupted to Balls Bridge by the early eighteenth century, is represented on the 1625 plan of Galway as having a span of four arches. This is probably incorrect as both the pictorial map (*11*) and the Phillips's prospect (1685) show it with three. The map

represents it as a solid stone structure with four cutwaters, which, allowing for certain artistic licence, would suggest that it had to cope with a significant flow of water. The river that flows beneath the bridge, known as Bald Bridge River (*1ᵉ1*), was considerably altered in the mid-nineteenth century when this stretch was incorporated into the newly constructed canal. A new swivel bridge was erected in 1851 on the site of the older structure, but with the decline in use of the canal this too needed to be replaced in the mid-twentieth century with a more permanent concrete form that still stands. The swivel bridge was last opened for traffic in 1954 to allow a 90-foot converted minelayer named Amo II to be brought to the sea.

32. BALLS BRIDGE

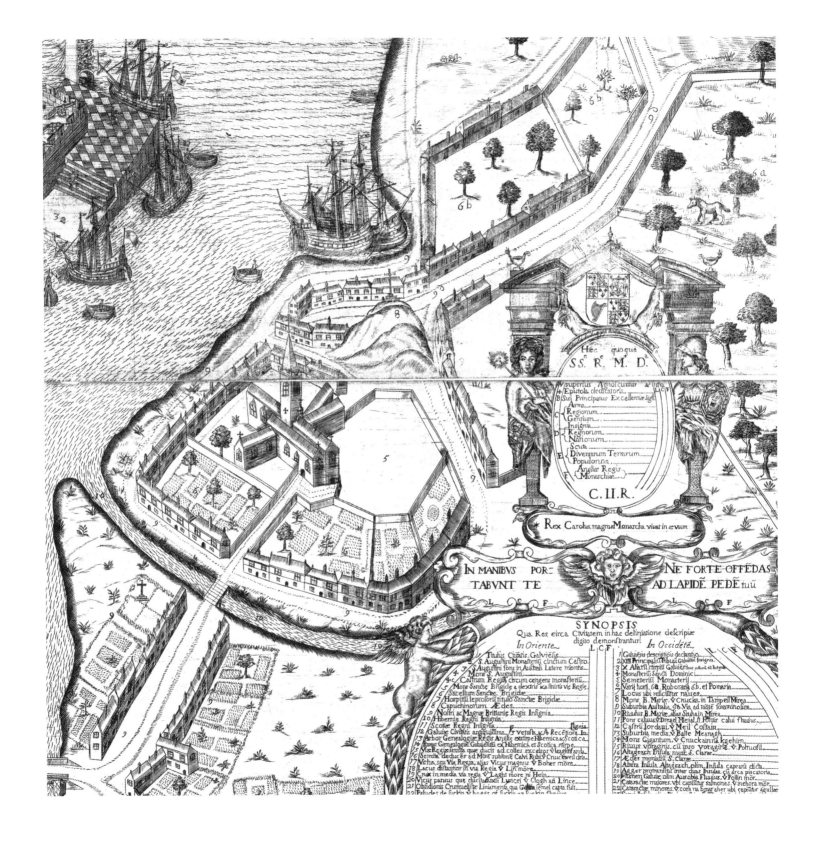

Hæc quoque
SS.ᵉ Rᵉ M.ᵈᵃ

C. II. R.

Rex Carolus, magnus Monarcha, viuit in ævum

IN MANIBVS POR- NE FORTE OFFÈDAS
TABVNT TE AD LAPIDĒ PEDĒ tuū

A Superius Agnoscitur & infra.
Å Epistola dedicatoria
B Sui Principatus Excellentia Signa
  Arma
C Regionum
  Gentium
  Insignia
D Regnorum
  Nationum
  Scuta
E Diversarum Terrarum
  Populorum
  Angliæ Regis
F Monarchiæ

SYNOPSIS
Qua Res circa Civitatem in hac deliniatione descriptæ
digito demonstrantur
In Oriente   In Occidēte

1 Tinitus Ciuitatis Galuiēsis.   1 Galuiēsis descriptiōis declaratio
2 S. Augustini Monasterii cinctum Castro.   2 XIII Principaliū Tribuū Galuiēsi Insignia.
3 Augustini fons in Australi latere montis. 3 X Aliarū stirpiū Galuiē, quæ adderi sit Insignia
4 Mons S. Augustini.   4 Monasteriū Sancti Dominici.
4 c Castrum Regis circum cengens monasteriū. 5 Semeterium Monasterii.
5 Mons Sanctæ Brigidæ, a dextris & a sinistris viæ Regis. 6 Varij horti, 6a Roborariā 6b. et Pomariā
6 Sacellum Sanctæ Brigidæ.   7 Locus ubi reficiuntur naues.
7 Hospitium leprosorū titulo Sanctæ Brigidæ. 8 Mons B. Mariæ, V Chucka in Tampell Mirea.
8 Capuchinorum Ædes.   9 Suburbia Australia, 9b Via ad mōte foraminosum.
9 Nostri & Magnæ Brittaniæ Regis Insignia. 10 Riuulus B. Mariæ, alias Sruhauā Mirea.
10 Hiberniæ Regni Insignia.   11 Pons caluus, Dread Meeal, ñ, Ponte caluo fluuius.
11 Scotiæ Regni Insignia.   12 Castrū Iordani, V Meil Costaiñ
12 Galuiæ Ciuitatis antiquissima, ♂ vetusta, & 4 Recētiora In Insignia. 13 Suburbia media, V Balle Meanagh
13 Arbor Genealogiæ Regis Angliæ exstirpe Hibernica & Scotica. 14 Mons Gigantum, V Cnuckain na ksehim.
14 Ramus Genealogiæ Galuiensiū ex Hibernica, et Scotica stirpe. 15 Riuus voraginis, cū ipso voragine, V Poltuosil.
15 Viæ Regiæ semita quæ ducit ad colles excelsos V Leaghin arda. 16 Altageach Insula münt S. Claræ.
16 Semita deduces ad Mōte sublime Calui Rubis V Cnuckweil cris. 17 Ædes monialiū S. Claræ
17 Vecha, seu Via Regia, alias Vicus magnus, V Boher mōr. 18 Altera Insula Altageach olim Insula caprarū dicta.
18 Lacus distantior in via Regia, V Liñ mōr. 19 Ager protensus inter duas Insulas, cū area piscatoria.
19 Crux in media via regia V Laght more ni Hein. 20 Flumen Galuiæ olim Ausobia Fluuius, V Pollin mōr.
20 Vicus paruus quæ ducit adlixit Lyncei V Clogh an Lince 21 Cataractæ maiores, ubi capiuntur salmones, V inchora mōr.
21 Obsidionis Crumuelistæ Liniamenta, qua Galuia semel capta fuit. 22 Cataractæ minores, V cora na bmar aher ubi capiūtur aquilæ.
22 Paludes de surkin V bogs of surkin ar surkin fluuius.

The details recorded on this map point to a settled and ordered suburb (*9*) – the area now known as the Claddagh. Its environment was suited not only to crafts associated with the repair of ships – referenced in the index but not numbered on the map where two vessels are shown beached on the shore – but was closely linked to the countryside. From its gardens (*6*), oak groves (*6ᵃ*) and orchards (*6ᵇ*) came raw materials for ship repairs and produce for the town's markets.

The origins of this suburb are traceable to at least the early thirteenth century when a small chapel, under the title of St Mary, was established there by the Premonstratensian canons of Tuam. At the close of the fifteenth century this chapel, then in ruins, was granted to the Dominicans of Athenry, who established a foundation here on the side of the hill called 'Blessed Virgin Mary Hill, commonly known as Cnochán Teampail Muire' (*8*). The topography of the hill has been exaggerated on the map – undoubtedly for emphasis – and the cross on its top, together with a smaller one in the back garden of a house to the east (left) of the road that leads from the friary to the town, add a further Christian dimension to this scene: neither cross is referenced in the map index.

In 1625 the friary was described as being surrounded by a great many houses and these are shown as almost completely encircling it, apart from the area outside its burial ground (*5*). The layout of these dwellings with their neat rear gardens (*6*) mirrors the topography of the river and the stream that flowed into it from the west. This stream, named Sruthán Muire (*10*), drained an area of marshland to the south-west and was reclaimed or culverted in the second half of the eighteenth century. To the south of the friary the road (*9ᵃ*) led to the Cave Hill (Cnoc an dolláin), the southern end of Fairhill.

At the time that this map was printed, the friary no longer existed. The buildings, which included a hospital or 'lasorous house', had been demolished in September 1651 with the assent of the Dominican community, lest they be used as a point for assault by the parliamentary army that was then encamped to the east of the town. Along with other religious the friars were forced into exile after the surrender of Galway in 1652, although a number returned and retained a vestigial presence in the neighbourhood of the town. The uneasy toleration that followed on the restoration enabled them to erect a new chapel in 1669 and, despite sporadic episodes of repression and expulsion in the eighteenth century, the Dominicans clung to their home where they have continued ever since in their support of the local Claddagh community.

The suburb's neat and ordered arrangement of two-storey dwellings presented on this map contrasts with the housing stock in this area of later centuries. Being the estate of a single family, the Whaleys, who had been granted extensive properties in Galway in 1660s, probably favoured its development as a cohesive community that by the late eighteenth and nineteenth centuries differed in so many ways from those within the walled town on the opposite side of the river. By then its economic and social character was centred on the fishing industry and on the building and repair of boats. Unfortunately, the Great Famine of the mid-nineteenth century, depleted fishing stocks and the advent of modern technology eventually sealed the Claddagh's fate as a separate community. The building of a bridge (on the site of the present Wolftone Bridge) in the middle of the nineteenth century contributed to its integration into the greater urban space, a process that finally was completed when its clusters and rows of cabins were swept away under a new housing scheme in the first half of the twentieth century.

Fig. 36: The Claddagh, photograph, *c.* 1930, showing the extent of estate prior to the demolition of houses. The large three-storey building on the right is the Dominican priory.

33. DOMINICAN FRIARY AND SOUTHERN SUBURB

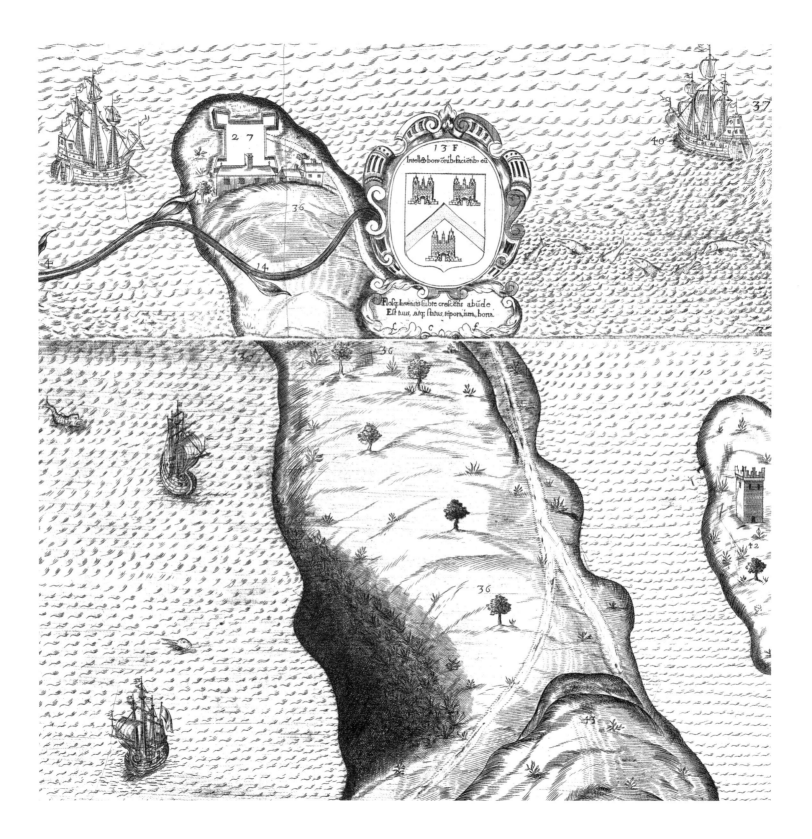

13 F
Intell& bonū ōrñ.bs.faciētib; eū

Flofq; Iuvēntis ſubte creſcētis abūde
Eſt tuus, atq; ſtatus, tēpora, iura, bona.

Attention has already been drawn (p. 4) to the fact that the inclusion on the map of a considerable amount of topographical detail in the hinterland of the town resulted in its distortion and contraction. Nowhere is this more evident than in the representations of the promontory of Rintinane (*36*) and Mutton Island (*42*). The promontory – in reality a narrow spit of land – curved around a large expanse of saltmarsh and mudflats that were covered at the spring tides. These mudflats (now reclaimed and forming South Park sportsground) have been constricted to a narrow band of dark shading on the map.

The placename Mutton Island points to a time when it was used as commonage for grazing sheep and the earliest form of the name, Enyskireach (the anglicised form of the Irish name Inis Caorach), dates to 1396 when the island is recorded as a boundary marker relating to the administration of custom duties for ships entering the port. By the early sixteenth century some form of navigational beacon had been erected there and this was described in 1602 as a 'small tower to control ships'. Given its strategic location in the bay (*37*), it was temporarily fortified some years later, but had been abandoned by 1637, when the island was recorded as devoid of any work save 'a waste turret of stone, built of purpose for a sea mark'. During the siege of Galway in 1651 a large party from one of the parliamentary ships (*40*) landed on Mutton Island and began to erect a fortification, but these were attacked by a force from the town that succeeded in killing all but one who managed to escape by swimming. Although the articles of surrender in 1652 mention the handing over of the 'forte on Mutton-island' no such work is included on the section of the island shown on this map. The neat battlemented tower depicted there can

Fig. 37: This watercolour sketch is titled 'Ruins of the old castle on Mutton Island' and dates to 1812. It represents the remains of works undertaken in the mid-eighteenth century that probably incorporated the earlier tower-structure shown on the map. This was converted in 1805 for use as a signal tower, which, together with the other works, was pulled down in 1815 to accommodate a lighthouse (GCCA, GS01/2).

probably be viewed as a further example of the compilers' desire to present a picture-perfect portrait of the town's built environment.

This statement also applies to the representation of the bastioned fort at Rintinane point (*27*), which was one of two such fortifications erected in 1643 by the townsmen to prevent relief reaching St Augustine's Fort, then under siege (see **24**). The remains of the second fort at Rinmore still survive and, while confirming the four-corner bastioned design, point to both as originally being constructed of earth without any stone facing (see also **27**). The houses represented on the map are confirmed in this location on Phillips's plan of 1685 where the fort is shown as an open square. By 1691 it had been converted to a fish palace for the processing and curing of herring.

34. MUTTON ISLAND AND RINTINANE FORT

The enclosed community of Poor Clare sisters who live on Nun's Island have had a continual presence in the town since 1642. In that year a group of twelve sisters and two novices travelled from their remote convent at Bethlehem, Co. Westmeath, to establish the new foundation in the town. Among them were four Galway women including Mary and Catherine Brown whose uncle, Martin Brown, is referenced on the map (see **19**).

At this time most religious orders were renting houses in the town and the sisters leased a dwelling in a lane (*67*) off present St Augustine Street close to the town wall (*K*). The demand for such accommodation was a boon to property owners, some of whom chose to capitalise on this situation by charging high rents. In 1649 the Poor Clare nuns petitioned the corporation for a site for their convent on account of 'the exorbitant rent they pay' and because their landlord was intent on evicting them when their lease was up. In their petition they requested 'sufficient room for building a monastery and rooms convenient thereunto, a garden and orchard, in the next island adjoining to the bridge of Illanalltenagh' (*16*). This island, together with that to the north-west (where the cathedral stands) were jointly known as Oileán Ealtanach and, according to the map index, the latter island was formerly named the 'island of goats'. The islands were linked by an embankment that also contained a 'fish tank' (*19*).

The corporation acceded to the community's request and, according to their own contemporary chronicler, the nuns built there a 'good large and spacious house with other conveniences' in 1650. It is very doubtful, given the unsettled times, that the finished buildings were as extensive as those illustrated on the map where a substantial church is depicted with Gothic-style windows and tracery (*17*). In consequence of their presence, this island would become known as Nun's Island.

After the surrender of Galway in 1652 the majority of the nuns, with many other religious, were forced into exile. A small number remained behind and went into hiding, staying with relatives or friends. Although their island was confiscated and granted to one of the new Cromwellian settlers, John Morgan, mayor of Galway in 1661–2, the nuns or their representatives appear to have entered into some form of accommodation with him as the few that remained were allowed to farm there and pay rent. Their determination and resourcefulness were called on again when the island, along with other

Fig. 38: Poor Clares' Lane (*67*) showing the house (*K*) rented by the Poor Clare sisters.

corporation possessions, was conferred by Charles II on one of his court favourites in 1673. On this occasion, one of the nuns travelled to London and obtained confirmation of their lease from the new owner. They then proceeded to make a garden and built a 'small lodge for such of the sisters as might want a change of air'.

In the aftermath of the Williamite war the community again was forced to disperse among relatives and friends and eventually moved into a large house in Market Street, the former town house of Sir Peter French (see **20**). In order to conceal their identity they set up a boarding school and, despite intermittent enforced expulsions, they continued to live there throughout the eighteenth century. In 1825 the Poor Clare sisters finally returned to Nun's Island and built a new convent and chapel, where they continue their enclosed contemplative life to this day.

35. POOR CLARE MONASTERY

Fish were not only a very important component in the diet of Galway households over the centuries but also provided significant revenue for those holding riparian rights or licences from the crown. Separate markets for both fresh- and salt-water fish are recorded on the map (*Elenchus*, m and q), the latter being held in front of the long-forgotten, but aptly named, Fishermen's Lane (*Elenchus*, 70) on the south side of Flood Street close to present Mayoralty House.

The salmon and eel fisheries, in particular, were important in that these species, being migratory, afforded greater scope for capture by the various devices available to fishermen at that time. Two fish weirs are recorded on the map, the Lesser Weir (*22*), or High Weir as it was also known, where eels were caught and the Great Weir (*21*) for catching salmon. Only a glimpse of the former is provided as it is almost totally obscured by the allegorical composition above the *Elenchus* table (see **3**). Both weirs are typical of the period in consisting of a number of hurdles of brushwood set in a V-shape in the river, with one or more cribs or nets at the apex of the V to trap fish either on their ascent (salmon) or on their descent (eels) of the river. Being entirely made of wood, the maintenance and upkeep of these weirs must have been demanding as they were easily damaged by floods or floating debris carried downstream.

The Lesser Weir, for catching eels, is shown with nets while the Great Weir has three cribs with curving wattle hurdles on the downstream side to trap salmon. Gaps were left at the eastern and western sides of the weir to allow a number of salmon return upriver to spawn, thus ensuring a

Fig. 39: The Lesser Weir (*22*) (top); a tidal fish trap at Whitestrand (bottom).

continuous supply for the following year's catch. A man is shown in the act of taking a salmon from one of the cribs by means of a spear: his successful catch lies at the bottom of the boat.

In addition to the two substantial weirs just mentioned, the map includes a fish-tank (see **35**) and depicts a tidal fish-trap on the shore to the west of the town close to where the southern extension of the stream known as Srúthán Muire (*10*) entered the sea at Whitestrand. Early seventeenth-century records document at least twenty other eel weirs on the river and numerous places above and below the West Bridge (see **11**) where fish could be caught with nets, spears and other devices.

The earliest documented reference to the Galway fishery dates to 1283 when it is listed as the property of Walter de Burgh, the principal founder of the town, who held it in right of a grant from the king. Over the centuries the fishery passed through numerous grantees and owners until it was purchased by the Irish state in 1978: it remains one of the most prolific salmon and eel fisheries in Ireland.

To the left (north) of the Great Weir is a rock (*14*) described in the index (under *Synopsis, in occidentem*, 24) as the place 'where, as it is said, the lady Galvia was drowned, whence the city was named'. This is one of the many mythological origin stories found in the collection of early Irish prose and poetry known as the Dinnseanchas. It is the stuff of literary invention and the more prosaic origin of the name Galway is that it derives from the Irish form Gaillimh, signifying a rocky or stony river.

36. THE GALWAY FISHERY

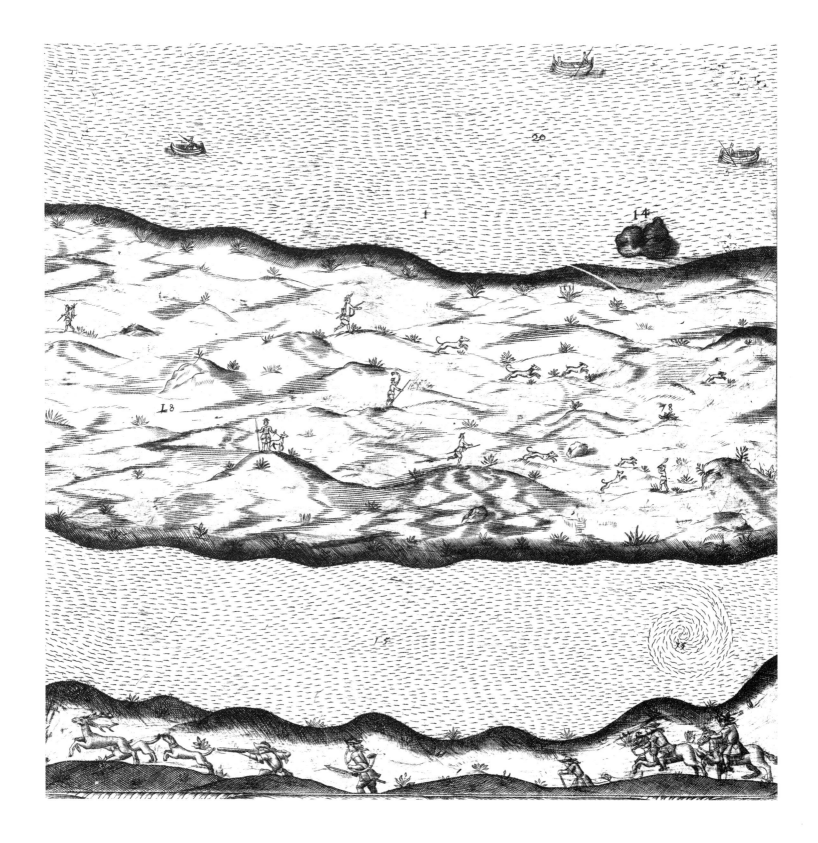

Hunting for game was evidently an important component in the life of the Galway inhabitants and five separate hunting scenes are represented on the map. A deer hunt is presented above the bottom border on the west side of the river in the hinterland of the town, while the pursuit of hares with a pack of hounds takes place on the eastern of the two islands known as the 'Islands of Altanach' (*18*), where the cathedral stands today, and also on the promontory of Rinmore. The fourth scene depicts the shooting of waterfowl in the pond or marshy area that was located at the depression in the highway of Bohermore, immediately south-west of the present cemetery (visible in **27**). In a lane to the north, alongside the Terryland River, another marksman takes aim at a fleeing hare, or perhaps, a rabbit.

Chasing deer with hounds was very much regarded as the noblest form of hunting, the sport of kings and favoured individuals, and its depiction on this map clearly is intended to testify to the high status of the townspeople. The deer hunt scene contains the full panoply of armed hunters, both mounted and on foot, accompanied by a pack of hounds. One of the huntsmen is armed with a spear and, as the horsemen carry

only pistols in their saddle holsters, they do not appear to be directly involved in the kill. Only one hunter is armed with a musket, which is very likely to have been a flintlock or 'snaphance' favoured by sportsmen as fowling pieces at this time. The hunter here prepares to fire his musket just as the hounds catch their quarry while his companion blows 'the mort' (i.e., the death) on his horn, a hunting call used to signal that the deer had been run down by the pack or killed. From earliest times the horn has been an integral part of the hunt and the curved examples depicted on the map remained in vogue until the middle of the seventeenth century when they were replaced, in England, by the straight hunting horn, a smaller version of which is still in use.

The success of the chase may be seen in the top left of the extract where the huntsman heads home with the catch hanging from his staff.

Fig. 40: Details from the various hunting scenes on the map.

37. HUNTING

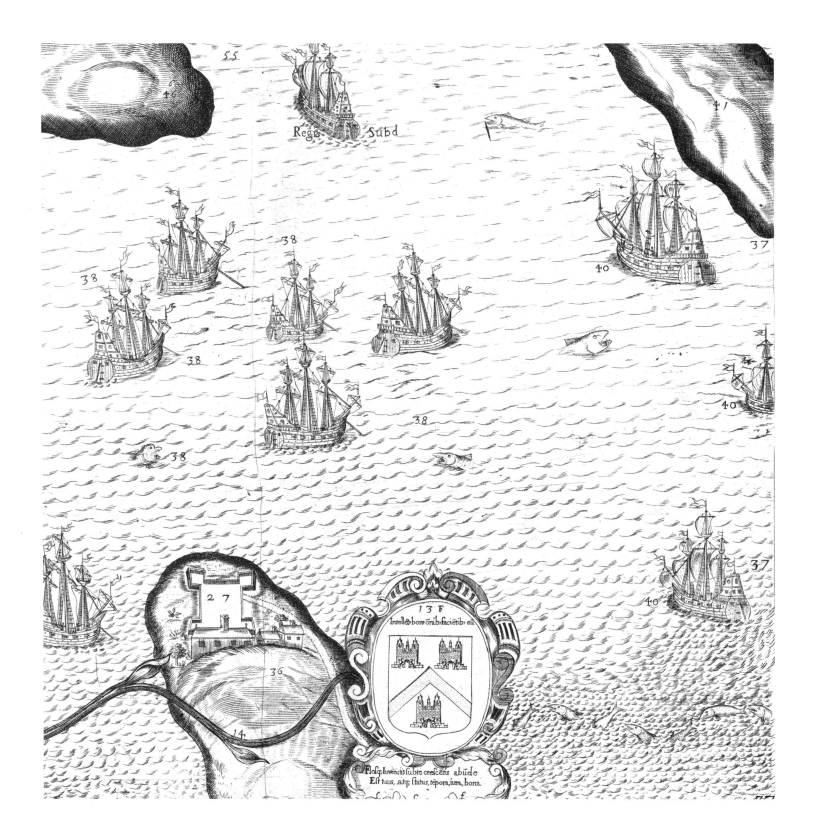

The compilers have included on the map numerous sea-going, in-shore and river craft by way of highlighting the town's internal and external trade networks while referencing also its maritime activities during the siege of 1651–2. Given that the map was engraved and printed in the Low Countries at a time when Dutch naval and mercantile power was at its height, one might expect that the representations of the vessels would correspond with those found in contemporary cartographical and marine art of the period. But this is not the case and the artist appears to have selected a stock ship image which, while displaying many of the characteristics and features of Dutch vessels, owes more to late sixteenth-century exemplars than to those in operation in the middle of the following century.

Fig. 41: A sailing boat with a leeboard navigates the waters in the area of the present docks.

wish the nationality or ownership of any vessel to be identified as the flags, ensigns, pennants and transoms (the usual location for the ship's emblem) are blank or bear only generic schematic devices.

Further evidence of Dutch influence is attested by the representation of the smaller in-shore craft and river boats and there is little doubt that the two boats with leeboards derive from stock cartographical images (see **7**, top left). In total, thirty-eight in-shore and riverine boats are depicted and most are engaged in typical everyday tasks: bringing goods and produce from the hinterland to the town (see **7**, top left); fishing (see **5**); tending weirs (see **36**); ferrying people (see **31**) or being tied up or released from a mooring (see **7**, top left). Only one lies empty at the water's edge (see **33**). Two vessels have a single sail and, although a small number are depicted with oars, the majority are shown as being propelled by a single individual using a long pole. This both suggests and confirms the shallowness of the Galway River and its immediate estuarine areas.

The majority of the thirty-two ships depicted are of a single generic type, a three-masted, square-rigged vessel. While providing the viewer with an appropriate display of merchantmen and men-of-war, the artist exhibits a distinct lack of knowledge of both sailing and rigging. The ships are depicted with a square rather than a lateen sail on the mizzen mast, have exceptionally high sterncastles – completely out of proportion to the vessel size – and all ships, whether sailing, anchored or moored have their yard hoisted high, a feature that was unusual for such vessels at this time.

To emphasise the map's Royalist narrative, three Cromwellian ships (*40*) – described as such in the map index – are shown 'pursuing the King's subjects to the port of Ardfry', a secure inlet on the south-east side of Galway Bay where the present Galway Bay Sailing Club is based (numbered 39 in the index table but incorrectly engraved as '*55*' on the map). Apart from using reference numbers to indicate these particular ships, it is evident that the compilers did not

In showcasing their safe harbour and bay the compilers have included a small section of Hare Island, named 'Ros Mór'(*4⁰6*), and another narrow band of land in the top right-hand corner of the map (*41*) that is described in the index as 'Part of the promontory of Rinn Mara': it has not proved possible to locate this promontory. Possible candidates are Ardfry Point or the western end of Tawin Island on the south side of the bay, but these are beyond the limits of the perspective employed for this section of the map. The depiction of a substantial shoal and the gaping mouths of large fish and other sea creatures breaking water – typical for maps of this period – not only draw the viewer's attention to the bay's bountiful harvest but point to the unknown, monstrous dangers of the deep.

38. MARITIME AND RIVER VESSELS

Andrews, J.H., *Maps in those days: cartographic methods before 1850* (Dublin, 2009).

Armstrong, E.C.R., 'The shields in the seventeenth-century map of Galway prepared for submission to the duke of Lorraine' in *JGAHS*, viii (1913–14), pp 235–6.

Ballon, Hillary and David Friedman, 'Portraying the city in early modern Europe: measurement, representation, and planning' in Woodward, *History of cartography, volume three*, pt 1, pp 680–704.

Blake, M.J., *Blake family records, 1600 to 1700: a chronological catalogue with copious notes and genealogies of many branches of the Blake family* (London, 1905).

Blake, M.J., 'Galway Corporation Book B' in *JGAHS*, v (1907–8), pp 65–144.

Blake, M.J., Caesar Litton Falkiner and W.F. Trench, 'Notes on the pictorial map of Galway' in *JGAHS*, iv (1905–6), pp 41–8.

Canny, Nicholas, 'Galway: from the Reformation to the penal laws' in Ó Cearbhaill, pp 10–24.

Coen, Martin, *The wardenship of Galway* (Galway, 1984).

Coleman, Ambrose, *The Irish Dominicans of the seventeenth century by Father John O'Heyne, O.P.* (Dundalk, 1902).

Cunningham, John, *Conquest and land in Ireland: the transplantation to Connacht, 1649–1660* (Woodbridge, 2011).

Duffy, E.P., 'Clanricarde and the duke of Lorraine' in *JGAHS*, xxxi (1964–5), pp 71–99.

Dutton, Hely, *A statistical and agricultural survey of the county of Galway, with observations on the means of improvement; drawn up for the consideration, and by the direction, of the Royal Dublin Society* (Dublin, 1824).

FitzPatrick, Elizabeth, Madeline O'Brien and Paul Walsh (eds), *Archaeological investigations in Galway city, 1987–1998* (Bray, 2004).

FitzPatrick, Elizabeth and Paul Walsh, 'Buildings and architecture' in FitzPatrick, O'Brien and Walsh, *Archaeological investigations in Galway city, 1987–1998*, pp 337–56.

Fleetwood Berry, James, *The story of St Nicholas' Collegiate Church, Galway* (Galway, 1912).

Gilbert, J.T. (ed.), 'Archives of the town of Galway' in *Historical Manuscripts Commission, tenth report* (London, 1885), app., pt v, pp 380–520.

Hardiman, James, *History of the town and county of the town of Galway from the earliest period to the present time* (Dublin, 1820).

Hardiman, James, 'The pedigree of Doctor Domnick Lynch, regent of the colledge of St Thomas of Aquin, in the city of Seville, A.D. 1674, from a coeval MS' in *Miscellany of the Irish Archaeological Society*, i (1846), pp 44–90.

Healy, Angelus, 'Some more dusty documents: "Wanderers for Christ"' in *The Capuchin Annual* (1935), pp 225–33.

Henry, William, *Roll of honour: the mayors of Galway city, 1485–2001* (Galway, 2002).

Henry, William, *Hidden Galway: gallows, garrisons and guttersnipes* (Cork, 2011).

Higgins, Jim, 'Galway city heritage survey' (5 vols, unpublished report of the Galway association of An Taisce quincentennial project, 1984).

Higgins, Jim, *Galway's heritage in stone. Galway City Museum, catalogue no. 1: late medieval sculpture down to the late seventeenth century in Galway City Museum* (Galway, 2003).

Higgins, Jim, *Galway's heritage in stone. Galway City Museum, catalogue no. 2: post-medieval and eighteenth–early twentieth-century sculpture in Galway City Museum* (Galway, 2004).

Higgins, Jim, *Galway's heritage in stone, catalogue no. 3: the stone carving collection at the National University of Ireland, Galway. A corpus of late-medieval and post-medieval sculpture from Galway city* (Galway, 2011).

Higgins, Jim and Susan Herringklee, *Monuments of St Nicholas' Church, Galway: an historical, genealogical and archaeological record* (Galway, 1992).

Jennings, Brendan, 'The abbey of St Francis, Galway' in *JGAHS*, xxii (1947), pp 101–19.

Johnson, David Newman, 'Lynch's Castle, Galway city: a reassessment' in Conleth Manning (ed.), *Dublin and beyond the Pale: studies in honour of Patrick Healy* (Dublin, 1998), pp 221–51.

Kavanagh, Stanislaus (ed.), *Commentarius Rinuccinianus de sedis apostolicae legatione ad foederatos Hiberniae Catholicos per annos 1645–1649* (6 vols, Dublin, 1932–49).

Koeman, Cornelis, Günter Schilder, Marco van Egmond and Peter van der Krogt, 'Commercial cartography and map production in the Low Countries, 1500–*ca.* 1672' in Woodward, *History of cartography, volume three*, pt 2, pp 1296–1383.

Koeman, Cornelis and Marco van Egmond, 'Surveying and official mapping in the Low Countries, 1500–*ca.* 1670' in Woodward, *History of cartography, volume three*, pt 2, pp 1246–95.

Leask, H.G., 'The collegiate church of St Nicholas, Galway' in *JGAHS*, xvii (1936–7), pp 1–23.

Leask, H.G., 'Doorway and window, St Augustine Street, Galway' in *JGAHS*, xviii (1938–9), pp 168–9.

Lynch, John, *Alithinologia sive verdica reponsio* [sic] *ad invectivam mendacijs, falacijs, calumniis ...* (St Omer, 1664).

Lynch, John, *De praesulibus Hiberniae, potissimis catholicae religionis in Hibernia, serendae, propagandae et conservandae authoribus*, ed. J.F. O'Doherty (2 vols, Dublin, 1944).

Lynch, John, *Pii antistitis icon or the life of Francis Kirwan, bishop of Killala* (St Malo, 1669; repr. Dublin, 1951).

MacLysaght, Edward (ed.), 'Report on documents relating to the wardenship of Galway' in *Analecta Hibernica*, no. 14 (1944), pp 7–186, 189–249.

Mac Niocaill, Gearóid, 'Medieval Galway: its origins and charter' in Ó Cearbhaill, pp 1–9.

Mac Niocaill, Gearóid, 'Medieval Galway: dependence and liberty' in H.B. Clarke (ed.), *Irish cities* (Dublin, 1995), pp 123–35.

Martyn, Adrian, *The tribes of Galway, 1124–1642* (Galway, 2016).

McCormack, Danielle, *The Stuart Restoration and the English in Ireland* (Woodbridge, 2016).

McErlean, John, 'Notes on the pictorial map of Galway: the index to the map' in *JGAHS*, iv (1905–6), pp 133–60.

McGowan, Brendan, *Eyre Square 300: aspects of its history* (Stroud, 2012).

McGrath, Bríd, 'Ireland and the third university: attendance at the Inns of Court, 1603–1650' in David Edwards (ed.), *Regions and rulers in Ireland, 1100–1650* (Dublin, 2004), pp 217–37.

McGrath, Bríd, 'Managing the Windsor of Ireland: the composition of Galway's town council, 1603–1653' in *JGAHS*, lxix (2017), pp 61–81.

Meehan, C.P. (ed.), *The portrait of a pious bishop; or, The life and death of the Most Rev. Francis Kirwan, bishop of Killala* (Dublin, 1884).

Millett, Benignus, *The Irish Franciscans, 1681–1685* (Rome, 1964).

Mitchell, James, 'Mayor Lynch of Galway: a review of the tradition' in *JGAHS*, xxxii (1966–71), pp 5–72.

Mitchell, James, 'The tholsel at Galway (1639–1822)' in *JGAHS*, xxxv (1976), pp 77–85.

Mitchell, James, 'The prisons of Galway: background to the inspector general's reports, 1796–1818' in *JGAHS*, ixl (1997), pp 1–21.

Moran, Gerard and Raymond Gillespie (eds), *Galway: history and society* (Dublin, 1996).

O'Brien, Celsus, *Poor Clares, Galway, 1642–1992* (Galway, 1992).

Ó Cearbhaill, Diarmuid (ed.), *Galway town and gown, 1484–1984* (Dublin, 1984).

O'Connor, John, *The Galway Augustinians. Volume 1. An abbey dies* (Galway, 1979).

O'Dowd, Peadar, *Old and new Galway* (Galway, 1985).

O'Dowd, Peadar, *Vanishing Galway* (Galway, 1987).

O'Dowd, Peadar, *Down by the Claddagh* (Galway, 1993).

O'Flaherty, Roderic, *A chorographical description of West or H-Iar Connaught, 1684,* ed. James Hardiman (Dublin, 1846).

O'Flynn, Thomas, *The Irish Dominicans, 1536–1641* (Dublin, 1993).

Ó Héideáin, Eustás (ed.), *The Dominicans in Galway, 1241–1991* (Galway, 1991).

Ó Máille, T.S., 'Place names from Galway documents' in *JGAHS*, xxiii (1948–9), pp 93–137; xxiv (1950–1), pp 58–70, 130–55.

Ó Máille, T.S., 'Ainm na Gaillimhe' in *Galvia*, i (1954), pp 26–31.

Ó Máille, T.S., 'Áitainmneacha na Gaillimhe' in Ó Cearbhaill, pp 51–2.

Ó Muraíle, Nollaig, 'Aspects of intellectual life in seventeenth-century Galway' in Moran and Gillespie, pp 149–212.

Ó Muraíle, Nollaig, *The celebrated antiquary: Dubhaltach Mac Firbhisigh (c. 1600–1671): his lineage, life and learning* (Maynooth, 1996).

O'Neill, Rose, *A rich inheritance. Galway Dominican nuns, 1644–1994* (Galway, 1994).

O'Riordan, Sean, 'Rinuccini in Galway, 1647–1649' in *JGAHS*, xxiii (1948–9), pp 19–51.

O'Sullivan, M.D., 'The lay school at Galway in the sixteenth and seventeenth centuries' in *JGAHS*, xv (1931–3), pp 1–32.

SELECT BIBLIOGRAPHY

O'Sullivan, M.D., 'The fortification of Galway in the sixteenth and early seventeenth centuries' in *JGAHS*, xvi (1934), pp 1–47.

O'Sullivan, M.D., *Old Galway: the history of a Norman colony in Ireland* (Cambridge, 1942; repr. Galway, 1983).

Ó Tuathaigh, Gearóid, 'Galway in the modern period: survival and revival' in H.B. Clarke (ed.), *Irish cities* (Dublin, 1995), pp 136–49.

Prunty, Jacinta and Paul Walsh, *Galway/Gaillimh* (Irish Historic Towns Atlas, no. 28, Dublin, 2016).

Schilder, Günter, *Monumenta cartographica Neerlandica* (9 vols, Amsterdam, 1986–2013).

Simington, R.C. (ed.), *Books of survey and distribution: being abstracts of various surveys and instruments of title, iii, County of Galway* (Dublin, 1962).

Travers, D. and M.J. Tighe (eds), *The Galliv. An illustrated history of the ancient city of Galway* (Galway, 1901).

Trench, W.F., 'Note on a doorway in Galway' in *JGAHS*, xvi (1905–6), pp 37–9.

Walsh, Paul, 'The foundation of the Augustinian friary at Galway: a review of the sources' in *JGAHS*, xv (1985–6), pp 72–80.

Walsh, Paul, 'The topography of the town of Galway in the medieval and early modern periods' in Moran and Gillespie, pp 27–96.

Walsh, Paul, *Discover Galway* (Dublin, 2001).

Walsh, Paul, 'The town walls and fortifications' in FitzPatrick, O'Brien and Walsh, *Archaeological investigations in Galway city, 1987–1998*, pp 309–36.

Walsh, Paul and Paul Duffy, 'An extract from Strafford's inquisition: Galway Corporation property in 1637' in *JGAHS*, xlix (1997), pp 49–64.

Went, A.E.J., 'The Galway fishery: an account of the ownership of the fishery' in *PRIA*, xlviii C (1942–3), pp 233–53.

Went, A.E.J., 'The Galway fishery: an account of the modes of fishing together with notes on other matters connected with the fishery' in *PRIA*, xlix C (1943–4), pp 187–219.

Woodward, David (ed.), *History of cartography, volume three: cartography in the European Renaissance* (2 pts, Chicago, 2007).

SELECT BIBLIOGRAPHY